· THE ·
WELL-ORDERED
OFFICE

*How to Create an Efficient
and Serene Workspace*

Kathleen Kendall-Tackett, Ph.D.

New Harbinger Publications, Inc.

Publisher's Note

This publication is designed to provide accurate and authoritative information in regard to the subject matter covered. It is sold with the understanding that the publisher is not engaged in rendering psychological, financial, legal, or other professional services. If expert assistance or counseling is needed, the services of a competent professional should be sought.

Distributed in Canada by Raincoast Books.

Copyright © 2005 by Kathleen Kendall-Tackett
New Harbinger Publications, Inc.
5674 Shattuck Avenue
Oakland, CA 94609

Cover design by Amy Shoup
Text design by Michele Waters-Kermes
Acquired by Tesilya Hanauer
Edited by Brady Kahn

ISBN 1-57224-385-6 Paperback

All Rights Reserved

Printed in the United States of America

New Harbinger Publications' Web site address: www.newharbinger.com

07 06 05

10 9 8 7 6 5 4 3 2 1

First printing

Contents

Welcome to the
Well-Ordered Office

Americans are working more than ever. And sometimes we waste time on the job. Procrastination, searching for lost items, background noise, and two-legged interruptions all decrease our productivity. The time that you spend at the office influences almost every aspect of your life—relationships, home, and health. Doesn't it make sense to use this time as efficiently as possible?

A couple of years ago, I read an article about office efficiency in an unlikely place—the journal *Science*. Picture, if you will, a group of scientists (pocket protectors optional). Is this a group you would expect to discuss, or even notice, office *decor*? And yet, the design of the scientists' labs actually influenced their productivity. Labs that worked well had flexibility, allowed for easy access to tools and equipment, and provided opportunities for congregating and "social interaction" (read: talking to each other). The layout and efficiency of the scientists' labs was directly related to their professional success.

My Story

Allow me to introduce myself. I am a health psychologist and work in a research lab at the University of New Hampshire. Much of my work revolves around helping people reduce the amount of stress in their lives, and stress in the workplace is a major issue. Workers at all levels strain under the yoke of too much to do in too little time. Downsizing has only compounded the problem.

In my travels, I've been in a wide variety of offices. While in school I worked as a clerical temp for several high-tech companies. I've worked in the business and service sector and in academics. I'm an administrator for two nonprofit organizations. I do regular consulting work. Through these experiences, I've had opportunities to observe a whole range of work situations. Some have been good; others needed some help. I've also discovered that when workers are inefficient, it affects everyone around them.

In my previous book, *The Well-Ordered Home*, I introduced four key principles to household organization. These principles are not only relevant to the workplace; many of them were actually *developed* there. Each one can help you use your time well. The principles are listed below:

- *Start where you are.* This first principle has to do with knowing who you are and how you like to work. It means working with, rather than against, your natural bent.

- *Have what you need.* In every work situation, there are tools that will make your job easier to do. Make sure that you have those tools and that they are where you need them.

- *Use active storage.* Active storage ensures that the tools you use most often are at your fingertips. It can help you make the most of even a small work space.

- *Get rid of clutter.* This final principle will encourage you to keep what you need and get rid of the excess. Every minute that you don't have to spend pawing through your mounds of clutter can be used more efficiently elsewhere.

Throughout this book, I will use the word "office" to refer to your work space, but I recognize that your work space may be a cubicle or desk in an open area. My suggestions apply to any of these configurations. Similarly, in most of my advice, I am assuming that you work in a setting outside your home, but these suggestions should be relevant even if you primarily work at home. While you may not need to deal with some of the interpersonal issues (such as office gossip—one of the key advantages to working at home), you will most likely have to deal with some of the other problems described here, such as interruptions or conflicting priorities. Suggestions about how to physically set up your work space apply to any office.

So come with me as we transform your work space and make you shine. Don't you deserve it?

PART I

Four Key Principles for a Well-Ordered Office

· 1 ·
Start Where You Are

I spoke with a reporter the other day who commented that she was pretty neat at home but that her office was often a disaster. It was, quite literally, her dirty little secret. As we chatted, I told her that I, too, am a messy worker, particularly when working on a big project. The difference between us was that I accepted, and even embraced, that aspect of myself. In fact, mess that appears on the surface can be deceptive (as can order). It is the underlying structure that makes a difference. As I learned to work with my natural style, I became more efficient and was also able to shrug off some of the "shoulds" that had limited me.

This can work for you too. Instead of trying to force a change, I propose that you start where you are. This means working with your natural bent and approaching your work knowing who you are and how you like to do things. Conversely, not starting where you are means fighting against yourself, making any task more difficult. Here are some examples.

What Happens When You Don't

You decide to color-code all your files and, in no time at all, lose track of what each color represents. Your color-coding scheme becomes far too complex to actually use. This process brings all your office filing to a screeching halt, and you end up worse off than when you started.

Or you spend a lot of money on an "office planner." This one even requires a special course to learn how to use it. The problem is that it weighs as much as a small child. You never carry it with you when you leave your desk, and so you never have it when you need it. So you jot items on sticky notes, gum wrappers, and other handy paper debris. Then you wonder why you keep losing track of your schedule.

How to Start Where You Are

The mistake you made in these situations was you were trying to use a tool or system that wasn't right for you. Don't make change a prerequisite for getting organized. Instead, ask yourself the following:

- *How do I prefer to do things?*

- *What skills and equipment do I already possess?*

- *Am I trying to force myself to do something?*

For example, unless you are a visual learner, a color-coded system is going to be difficult for you. Similarly, this system is going to be hard if you don't know the two to three categories (at the most) that you need. Whatever filing system you choose, it needs to be one that makes intuitive sense to you. This way, it will be easy to implement and maintain.

Along these same lines, a planner that is not with you most of the time is not going to be useful—especially if you are frequently away from your desk. So think of what you could carry around. I have a senior colleague who for years carried all of his important information in a spiral notebook in his pocket. His system was not fancy, but it served him well throughout much of his long career.

Next time you get stuck, ask yourself whether you are starting where you are. In almost every case, the answer to any organizational dilemma will come by working with, rather than against, your natural bent.

· 2 ·
Have What You Need

I have a confession to make. I love office supplies. I love finding items that will make my work easier or make my office a more pleasant place to be. Perhaps you do too. Having the office supplies you need is principle number two.

I've discovered that people are often woefully short of items that they need for working at home. This tends to be less true in offices. However, even in your office, you may be missing tools that you need. It's helpful to think about the different types of work you do. Here are some examples. These are just suggestions, and you can adapt them to fit the needs of your work situation.

Telephone Supplies

In almost every type of job, chances are you will use a telephone from time to time. To make this office tool work well, you need to always keep paper and pens nearby. You need phone books and any specialized directories near your phone (not across the room). If you are like me, you may have quite a few. I have about eight directories (from different organizations) at any given time. For a long time, I had them in a random pile. Then, one day, it occurred to me to put them in a notebook with sheet protectors. Now they're easy to find and use. I update these as I get more current information.

Paper-Producing Supplies

If you are in charge of ordering your own supplies, make sure that you always have paper and printer supplies (toner or inkjet cartridges). Running out during some crucial project produces needless amounts of stress. As soon as you install the last cartridge in your printer, or you open your last ream of paper, it's time to get more.

Paper-Handling Supplies

Handling paper is one of the biggest components of most office jobs. Make sure that you have the supplies you need to handle paper with ease. Paper-handling supplies include letter openers, box openers, stapler and staples, staple removers, paper clips, rubber bands, glue sticks, correction fluid, pens, pencils, a pencil sharpener, a ruler, notepaper, sticky notes, and scissors. You also need a place to put incoming items, a place for outgoing items, and a place for items to be filed.

Mail Supplies

If you handle your own mail, you will need envelopes in various sizes: letter, 5 by 8, 8½ by 11. You will also need mailing labels, stamps of various values, a postage scale, a felt-tip marker, packing tape, and boxes and supplies from the U.S. Postal Service, FedEx, UPS, or other carriers you use. Store these together, too, preferably in a place where it is easy to assemble packages for mail.

The items I've just described are the basics. Perhaps you already have these supplies, but they are scattered throughout your office. Maybe your staff takes care of these things for you. While it is wonderful to have a staff, it is ultimately in your best interest for you to be as efficient as possible. I know several people who have never worked outside their professions and are therefore clueless about how their office works. I find that they're at a disadvantage. Don't let this happen to you! Make sure that you have the equipment you need. In the next chapter, I'll help you think about the best place to put it.

· 3 ·
Use Active Storage

The next principle originated in the workplace, and you may find it one of the most helpful suggestions that I offer. At the turn of the twentieth century, a man by the name of Fredrick W. Taylor conducted a number of time-and-motion studies on factory assembly lines. He began by observing the actions of people who were already efficient on the production line and making painstaking observations as they went about their work. Based on his observations, he set up work spaces so that people could do their work with as little wasted effort as possible. And productivity increased.

Alas, this story did not have a happy ending. He got the labor unions to agree to his methods when he pointed out that increased productivity would benefit everyone and workers would share in the profits. Unfortunately, this is not how it turned out. Manufacturers loved the increased productivity, but they didn't share the profits. The unions protested, and eventually all time-and-motion testing was banned from the workplace. "Taylorization" became a malediction, meaning overly regimented, restrictive, and noncreative.

But Taylor was on to something, and what he discovered survives to this day. One of his most powerful principles was that of *active storage*. This means that you keep the items you need most frequently at hand. Items you use less frequently can be placed in less accessible spaces. This eliminates that paw-and-thrash time that accompanies a lot of office work. Here's how to go about it.

- *Have your telephone supplies near your telephone.* Even if you have a portable phone, having your supplies where you usually talk on the phone will save time when it comes to taking messages or jotting notes.

- *Have your paper supplies nearby.* Wherever you produce and handle paper, you'll need your paper supplies nearby. Handling paper also means handling files. So have your file folders, hanging folders, and labeler nearby. Also, wherever you keep your files should be within arm's reach. Files that you refer to frequently should be in the drawers (or containers) near you. Files that you only access some of the time can be farther away.

- *Keep mailing supplies handy.* After you've assembled the mailing supplies described in chapter 2, put them together in a place where they are easy to reach. This can be in bins or on stacking shelves on a work surface. If you are tight on space, you can keep them together in a container to pull out as needed.

By having all these items available and at your fingertips, you'll save minutes during every part of your workday. And these minutes can add up to hours by the end of the week. Perhaps more important, you'll save aggravation because you won't always be frantically searching for things. Your workday will be calmer, and you'll be more efficient, to boot.

· 4 ·
Get Rid of Clutter

We had a problem in our lab. For years, our offices were too small. Toward the end of our crisis, the staff was actually stowing supplies under and around its desks. The result was chaos. It was a miracle that anything got done (and it did, due largely to the staff's extraordinary efforts).

Then an amazing thing happened. Approximately half our staff moved to a new building. Suddenly, the clutter was gone. Several of the associates told me that they were much more efficient and that it seemed easier to get their work done. This experience demonstrated that in work spaces, less is definitely more. Clutter cuts down on efficiency and adds to everyone's stress level. When packed together, the women in our office were having a much harder time getting their work done because of all the extra stuff lying around.

So what are some of the common types of clutter?

Paper Clutter

In almost any office, paper makes up the majority of the clutter. Current estimates are that the average person handles about 660 pounds of paper per year. If you do not learn to handle your office paper well, it can soon bury you. What starts as an innocent-looking pile soon multiplies until you have no place to sit or no surface that is free from piles of paper.

Furniture and Equipment

Too much furniture and equipment can also be a major form of clutter. This can also include old computers, broken equipment, and odds and ends of furniture that make it difficult to walk around. Clutter can also include out-of-date software (and the nice shiny manuals!) or equipment that you are not currently using. Even if everything you have in your space is good and functional, you may still have too much of it to work efficiently.

Personal Items

Personal items can become a source of clutter. I think it's nice to have some. I have a large collection of snow globes, magnets, and postcards from my various travels and a few stuffed animals (including a very important University of New Hampshire cow that I just had to have). But I'm in research and generally don't meet the public. Depending on the situation, personal items may be inappropriate. For example, I'd be a tad concerned if I walked into any doctor's office (other than a pediatrician) and found a bunch of stuffed toys. Similarly, you probably wouldn't want to see snow globes atop the desk of your investment banker or family attorney. And if your work space is in a public area, you may also need to keep personal items to a minimum. As a general rule, I'd limit their number based on the needs of your office and whether these items are impairing your work. If you can't use your desk because it is overloaded with your things, then it is time to thin the herd.

Clutter can make any part of your work more difficult. It is stressful to walk into an office groaning under a load of stuff. In subsequent chapters, I'll show you how to deal with paper, office equipment, and time wasters that are choking your work space. But, for now, start looking at your office with a critical eye. Are there some things you should retire, pass along, recycle, or throw away? Have some items come to rest in your office that do not belong there? And is it time to take a few things home?

PART II

Organization Begins in Your Mind

▪ 5 ▪
If Your Date Book Could Talk: Why Personal Organization Matters

In my professional life, I constantly have to coordinate schedules with other academics. It is a bit like herding cats. I edit books where individual authors from around the country contribute chapters, and I coordinate two conferences every year, which means gathering materials from speakers.

In these two facets of my work, I need items delivered to me within a certain time frame. And I often have clues about whether the person I'm dealing with is going to make the deadline or going to miss it. I can tell a lot by how people keep their personal space and possessions. For example, when I see a date book with a two-inch pile of paper scraps, sticky notes, business cards, receipts, and other debris, I realize that this person is probably overwhelmed and will need more regular reminders about the work he or she has promised.

How we comport ourselves speaks loudly about who we are and how we do things, and people talk to each other. Every work situation I've ever been in has had an office grapevine. People know who is disorganized and who is not. By and large, people prefer working with organized people.

The reason for this is pretty straightforward—disorganized people waste everyone's time. This doesn't mean that they are bad people. Often, they are quite nice. But it can be frustrating and stressful to work with people who always miss (or completely forget about) deadlines, or who always need to be chased to get their promised work, or who are always a whirl of inefficient activity. Coworkers and colleagues become frustrated when disorganized coworkers waste their time or make them work extra hours to meet a dead-line. Important jobs fall through the cracks and don't get done. Given a choice, most people opt to work with people who are on top of their work and get things done in an orderly way.

Date books are not the only things that can talk. How we keep our desks, or briefcases, or even our cars tells a lot about us. So what does this mean for you? It can mean that when people see your messy spaces, fair or not, they may be making negative assumptions about you. In addition, date books and other items can be barometers of personal stress. People with messy personal spaces are often the most stressed out, and their lives seem completely out of control. This can influence your relationships both on and off the job, for it is often easy to snap at others when you feel overwhelmed.

The good news is that learning to be organized can influence every part of your life for the better. But first, you must listen. What are your date book, briefcase, desk, and car saying to you? Look at them with a fresh eye, not one that's used to seeing the clutter and mess. You may be well-organized in some areas. Other areas may need some improvement.

I find that when I start having lots of little notes and "to do" lists lying about, it's time to stop and regroup. Afterward I'm in the frame of mind where I can concentrate, once again, on my work. Even small changes can lower your stress level and improve the quality of your life. The first step is up to you.

• 6 •
Thoughts That Sabotage Organization

What you think can influence how organized you are. Conversely, thought patterns can keep you in chaos and keep you from reaching your goals. The good news is that you can control your thoughts. Once you recognize dysfunctional patterns, you can address them.

Thoughts to Avoid

Here are some of the most common types of thoughts that can undermine your organizational efforts.

Perfectionism. Some people refuse to make changes in their lives unless they can do things "perfectly." I've seen people with their offices in total disarray who seem paralyzed by their inability to live up to their impossible goal.

All-or-nothing thinking. This belief is strongly related to perfectionism. It's that little voice in your head that taunts you with "Do you think this is making any difference at all? Look at all the mess you still have to clean up." It mocks any of your efforts to take small steps. This type of thinking can also stop you cold.

Shame. I've met a lot of men and women who feel a great deal of shame about the state of their offices, homes, and lives. Shame is the voice that says you are stupid, lazy, or a slob. It makes you want to avoid the whole thing. Shame can also mock any of your initial first steps to make positive changes in your life.

Feeling that "clerical" work is not worth your time. Something I've observed for years, and it mystifies me, is when people think they are too smart, or are at too high a level professionally, to do anything that smacks of clerical work—even when that work involves taking care of their own correspondence or filing. So, like mandarins, they refuse to learn how to do their own office work. If you have this belief, it is not in your best interest. Since the trend in business is toward eliminating ancillary positions, you may have to do this work yourself, anyway, in the near future.

What to Do

Once you recognize these unhelpful thoughts, you can take some steps to counter them.

Recognize them. Destructive thoughts are often in the background of our awareness. The first step is to recognize that they exist.

Challenge them with truth. Ask yourself whether your unhelpful thoughts are really true. For example, does everything have to be perfect to be worthwhile?

Address the difficulties. If there is a specific problem, how can you handle it? For example, if you tend toward all-or-nothing thinking, start small and create pockets of organization within your office. Even having one really organized, neat drawer can be inspiring. As you start with small victories, in a short time you will see compelling evidence that your efforts are making a difference.

Recognizing and dealing with thoughts that sabotage your efforts can bring you closer to organizing your work space. You might even find that other areas of your life benefit when you shut off your internal critics.

▪ 7 ▪
How to Stop Procrastinating

You know the feeling. That pile of paper looms large. You feel guilty. Your palms sweat. You try to push dealing with it out of your mind. So the pile sits, and soon it is joined by its brethren. Eventually you have paper all over the office.

Procrastination. It's so easy to do. Everyone does it at least some of the time. But too much procrastination can be a problem. It can create stress, affect your job performance, and occupy a lot of brain time. While you are procrastinating, you may think about a task four or five times longer than it actually takes to do. What a waste! As common as procrastination is, there are also some easy ways for you to beat it.

Identify Tasks That Make You Procrastinate

This may seem obvious, but sometimes we are not even aware of our procrastination. Step one is to start noticing which parts of your work you never seem to have time for.

Try to Figure Out Why It Is Hard

People procrastinate for lots of different reasons. Perhaps you don't know how to do the task you've been dreading. Maybe it's too much to do alone, and it feels like punishment. Perhaps it involves a type of work that you find particularly challenging.

Address Difficulties

Once you've figured out why something is hard or unpleasant for you to do, think about ways you can make it easier. Here are some suggestions:

- *Make sure all the tools you need are handy.* Following the principle of "have what you need," make sure that everything you need to do the job is at hand. Having to go search for some item will bring your efforts to a screeching halt.

- *Get technical support.* If you don't know how to do something, ask around and find someone who can help. If possible, don't wait until the last minute to bring someone else on board.

- *Get moral support.* A new or dreaded task can be daunting to try alone. If you're dreading a task, ask a friend or coworker to sit with you while you work. Even if this person does not have technical knowledge, he or she can be nearby to offer moral support. Be sure to do the same in return.

- *Assess whether your total workload is realistic.* Sometimes we stall on getting something started because we just have too much to do. If that's the case, you may need to redistribute your workload, seek assistance, or push back some of your deadlines.

- *Work at your peak time of day.* Sometimes, the best time to tackle a project you've been dreading is first thing in the morning, when your mind is clearest. Whatever time is good for you, make sure that everything you need is assembled, so you can begin right away.

Even though lots of people procrastinate, learning to conquer this tendency can help in many areas of your life. It will lower your stress level and make your work more pleasant to do. It's something positive you can do for yourself every day.

• 8 •
One Bite at a Time: Little Steps Mean a Lot

The book you're reading is my tenth. You would think that, by now, it would be easy for me to start writing a book. But to be honest, I've had trouble starting each and every one of them. In pondering this, I've realized that it is hard to start because, at the beginning, the task before me looks impossible. As I face the task of producing three hundred, five hundred, or seven hundred pages, the pitiful three pages I've produced so far seems, well—pitiful.

I've noticed that many people facing a large task often feel the same way. The task is so big, and what you've done so far seems so small. Running away starts looking like a great option. Organizing your office may seem this way to you. If that's the case, I've got some good news. There are strategies that can get you past that initial hurdle.

- *Recognize the feelings that keep you from getting started.* First, you must acknowledge to yourself that you are nervous about starting. Once you acknowledge that fact, you can get support and move on to the next step.

- *Break the jobs into small parts.* Take a big job and break it down. One of the most helpful ideas I've stumbled across is the idea of a writing schedule that will break my job into small bits. I figure out how many days or weeks I have until something is due; then I calculate the number of chapters or pages that need to be done each day or week. It's not very creative, but it gives me a visible measure of progress that keeps me from having panic attacks in the beginning. You can divide most jobs that you have to do in a similar way.

- *Reward yourself for reaching small goals.* Especially in the beginning, be sure to give yourself small rewards for reaching your goals. It might mean taking a little time off to take a walk, have lunch with a friend, or buy a good book. (Be careful with snack rewards, or you may end up with another problem. Trust me on this.) Make your reward something you would really enjoy. This can often spur you to take the first step.

- *If necessary, remove the total from your sight.* My husband learned the value of doing this when he was fresh out of college and supervising three shifts on the manufacturing floor of a printed circuit board company. One of the first problems he faced was the massive backlog of boards that needed to be tested. They were in huge piles around the room, where they discouraged everyone. His strategy? Move the boards to another room and bring out a few at a time. In fairly short order, the crews had caught up on their backlog. You may find that removing your pile, or whatever you need to organize, will increase your motivation. My only caution would be to make sure that you don't just forget about the pile you have moved out of sight. Consider enlisting the cooperation of a coworker who can bring you a portion to work on every day.

So, thinking about your office, let's say you have a large pile of accumulated correspondence that needs filing. You could handle, say, an inch of papers or perhaps the contents of two folders' worth each day. As you make progress, you may find that your work goes faster and faster.

I think you'll be surprised at how quickly your accomplishments accumulate over time. Even organizing enough to save ten minutes a day can mean almost an hour every week. Start small, and see how far you can go.

· 9 ·
Setting Up Efficient Work Spaces

Most office spaces are set up with work in mind. That's the good news. The bad news is that even when the basic structure is good, your work space still can be pretty inefficient. Luckily, it doesn't have to stay this way. Throughout this book, I'll offer suggestions for specific parts of your office, such as your filing cabinet or desk drawers. For now, though, I want you to think about your work space as a whole.

Start with What You Have

Recognize, right up front, the strengths and limitations of your work space. Often, the problem is that you are trying to do too many things in too little space or the equipment you need is not readily available.

Note Any Changes That Are Feasible

You might be able to move furniture that you don't need. Can you clear off any surface areas? Are there files that you don't need to refer to that can be archived somewhere else?

Consider the Quality of Your Environment

The next consideration is the overall environment of your office.

- *Lighting.* Is the lighting adequate? Eyestrain is a common problem in the workplace. For example, a computer monitor near a window is a prescription for eyestrain, as is close work in inadequate light. Make sure that you have adequate task lighting and are not dealing with glare.

- *Temperature.* Another environmental consideration is temperature. Battles over temperature can arise, especially in a large office area. Some people like the office toasty and warm, while others think chilly is ideal. Think about what you can do to make yourself comfortable while you work (such as bringing a sweater or a fan from home).

- *Air quality.* Unfortunately, people can often become sick from breathing the air in their office buildings. There are fumes from carpets, fabrics, and paint. There is recycled air, perfume, and cigarette smoke. If you are prone to chemical sensitivity or upper respiratory infections, consider getting a portable air filter for your office. Adding plants can also help with air quality.

- *Noise.* Noise can also be a major source of distraction and can increase the stress of your workday—especially if you are in the center of a large office bull pen. In chapter 42, I'll give you some specific strategies to deal with noise. For now, make note of what your daily noise level is.

- *Comfort.* Repetitive strain injuries, such as carpal tunnel syndrome or neck injuries, are common among office workers. Make sure your desk and table height are such that you are not hurting yourself as you go about your daily work.

Your office setup can have a dramatic influence on your daily stress level and efficiency. Think about what you need to make your office a pleasant and productive place to be.

· 10 ·
The Serenity Prayer in the Workplace

God give me the serenity to accept things which cannot be changed;
Give me courage to change things which must be changed;
And the wisdom to distinguish one from the other.

I'll never forget my first encounter with this prayer. I was in high school and saw it written on a plaque. It struck me as incredibly wise advice. It still does. It is, of course, the Serenity Prayer, which is used all over the world in twelve-step programs.

Part II of this book has focused on some of the mental work that needs to be done as you bring your office into order. How the Serenity Prayer relates to your work may not be obvious, but there is a connection. Let's start with the first line—accept things that cannot be changed. At some point in our lives, we all need to recognize that there are certain aspects of our lives that we have no control over. They may be part of our personality or makeup; they may be our natural aptitudes and abilities. For example, I know that I will never (ever) be good at accounting. This is a limitation, but I can work around it.

Accepting what you cannot change can also apply to your coworkers. Twelve-step programs do an excellent job of teaching that you cannot change other people; all you can change is yourself. I knew a woman several years ago who vehemently hated her boss. Every time I would see her, she would recount, in vivid detail, his latest "sins" against humanity in general and against her in particular. Her therapist finally told her that she needed to either make her peace with this man or look for another job. You may come to a similar place with a boss or coworker.

The second line of the prayer asks for courage to change things that you can. It makes sense to try to improve any area of your life that is under your control, and you probably control much more than you think. Even if, for example, you are unable to increase the size of your work space, there is probably a lot you can do to make it function better. Or you can just sit around and complain. Personally, I would rather do something. I hope the same is true for you.

Courage may also be required when you need to make a change. When the querulous coworker or boss becomes abusive, or you finally recognize that his or her behavior is abusive, it takes great courage to seek out a better situation. It takes courage to realize that you may need to go back to school to update your skills. It also takes courage to be more organized after years of calling yourself a "slob."

Finally, it takes considerable wisdom to recognize what is controllable in your work situation and what is beyond your control for example, you may take responsibility for the actions or behaviors of other people when, in reality, they are not within your control. Conversely, you may fail to see how you can make some situations better. With experience, you will learn how to make the distinction. With each obstacle you face, always ask yourself, "What *can* I do?" It might help for you to write down the changes you would like to make. Within a fairly short time, you will discover that there are often many things you can do to improve your situation. And the things you can't change may spur you to move on to new territory. Either way, you can't lose. Serenity will be icing on the cake.

▪ 11 ▪
Make the Most of What You Have

In 1997, I was diagnosed with lupus. It was my surprise entry into the world of disability. At times, this experience has been difficult. What suprised me was the number of positives this experience would bring into my life. Disability has forced me to think about my life in a different way. I simply must adapt my work so that I can be maximally effective. What I've learned can help you too. Even without a disability, you may need to adapt your work situation to be your most effective. Sometimes limitations can be the catalyst for creative solutions.

Take a Personal Inventory

Perhaps the first step is to realistically assess where you are. All of the factors I've listed below can influence your productivity and how you feel about yourself and the work you do.

- *Type of work.* What types of work do you excel at? What types are difficult? Is your current job a good match for your abilities?

- *Attention level.* What is your attention level? Can you concentrate, or are you easily distracted by the goings-on around you? What is your optimum noise level? (Dead silence can be highly distracting for some.) Do you often leave a job half-finished because something else distracted you? Do you have attention-deficit/hyperactivity disorder or a similar condition? This is discussed further in chapter 12.

- *Introversion/extroversion.* Do you work better alone or with others? Are you an introvert or extrovert? Or, to put that question another way, do you get exhausted (introvert) or energized (extrovert) by your contact with others?

- *Energy level.* When is your energy and concentration level the highest? When is it at a low?

Create an Environment Where You Can Win

Once you have taken a realistic look at your strengths and weaknesses, you are then poised to be at your best. Consider these possibilities:

- *Time of day.* If you are at your best in the morning, make sure that you do your most challenging tasks then. You could prepare everything you need the day before so that you can hit the ground running in the morning. If your energy lags in the middle of the day, look for ways to eat a healthy snack (just like Mom used to recommend!), and maybe take a ten-minute walk. Both of these strategies will boost your energy level.

- *Noise level.* If you are highly distracted by noise, take some steps to counter it. You might even need to go somewhere else for a period of time when you need to concentrate.

- *Disability.* If you are working with a disability or attentional issue, think about ways that you can adapt your work situation to meet your needs. Do you need more structure? Do you need some kind of periodic reminder? Do you need some adaptive equipment?

You may be embarrassed by your need to be different and, as a result, refrain from making these types of changes. I suggest you focus on the benefits you bring *because* of your differences. Embrace these, learn to work with them, and realize that you have a positive contribution to make.

▪ 12 ▪
Driven to Distraction: How Attentional Issues Can Lead to Office Mess

A few months ago, I read an interesting article about attention-deficit/hyperactivity disorder (ADHD) in women. It said that Attention Deficit Disorder (ADD) or ADHD is frequently overlooked in girls because they are less likely to be hyperactive than boys. As a result, adult women frequently don't realize that they have it. The author described how women often only realize that they have ADD/ADHD when their children are diagnosed.

I found the topic interesting for personal reasons. One of my sons has been having difficulties in school, and consequently, my husband and I have become a lot more aware of our own learning styles. One thing that I've noticed is my own level of distractibility. In fact, we often joke about having "ADHD moments." Left to my own devices, I've been known to wander off and leave quite a few half-finished projects in my wake. I've also found that this tendency is directly related to the neatness of my working and living spaces. I know I'm not alone.

As I mentioned earlier, I am a messy worker. When I really get moving on something, I will often have books open on every surface. When I'm finished with something, I've been known to toss items, such as books or journals, across the room (gently, watching out for others) so that they are near where I need to put them away. My notes can be messy. I even keep several computer files open at once, so I can go back and forth between them. It's quite obvious how my attentional issues can lead to messiness. Many other people I meet have a very similar style. They are often embarrassed by it. I'm not, because I know I can still be quite productive. Plus, I'm more likely to be productive if I don't try to make myself be neat at every step along the way. Meanwhile, I've found some strategies that help.

- *Keep a project tracking list.* I've found it absolutely essential to keep a list tracking projects that are in progress. Otherwise, it is very easy for me to become so absorbed in one project that I forget about all the others. Even so, I still become absorbed, but I try to limit it to a few hours (or days) at a time.

- *Take time to regroup.* Even the self-identified messy person will get to the point where it is time to stop and tidy up. When my desktop is completely covered, or when I am frantically searching for something that was *right there*, I know it is time to stop, put a few things away, and maybe have a snack.

- *Have good underlying structure.* Another strategy that helps is to have good overall office organization. That way, the surface may be messy, but you can stop and put things away with ease.

- *Music may help.* A friend recently pointed out that people with attentional issues often find that music with a steady beat helps them concentrate. Some background music may help focus your attention. Experiment with different types of music to see if it helps.

- *Accept yourself.* Lots of people have attentional issues, including some really brilliant ones. Oftentimes, men and women with attentional issues go through school and life feeling bad about themselves. If you have an attentional issue, it's important to accept and accommodate it. You might also realize that your ability to hyperfocus or to switch between projects can be an advantage at times.

· 13 ·
Maximizing Your Creativity

One of the most useful classes I ever took was The Psychology of Creativity. The professor, Teresa Amabile, now at Harvard Business School, has spent most of her career researching creativity. You may think creativity is only relevant to "creative types," such as artists or musicians. In fact, creativity is highly important in all types of work. A company with employees who can think outside the box is more likely to thrive when others are barely hanging on. So, what are some things that can kill creativity in the workplace? Here is a summary of what Terri Amabile has found in her studies.

Lack of autonomy. When people don't have control over what they do and how they do it, they are less likely to come up with creative solutions.

Frequent interruptions. A workday that is constantly interrupted lowers creativity. Meetings, phone calls, and e-mail can all be sources of interruptions.

Not having the right tools or resources. Not having the tools, equipment, or resources you need can hamper your creativity.

Time pressure. Despite what you might think, creativity cannot flourish under constant time pressure. While time pressure can break through procrastination, deadline pressure keeps you from taking risks—and that limits creativity.

Hierarchical or rigid management structure. Collaborating with others is a great way to become more creative. When everyone is protecting his or her own turf, however, there are few chances for creativity.

Fear of failure. Being afraid to make mistakes can also kill creative approaches. Some of this fear may come directly from the milieu of your job. It may come from your misguided beliefs about the need to always be perfect. Either way, it can be harmful.

What You Can Do

There are some steps you can take to increase your creativity in the workplace.

- *Be proactive.* In order to counteract areas where you lack autonomy, try to figure out what you do have control over, and start there. People don't perform well when they are micromanaged. If this continues to be a problem, you may need to have a frank talk with your manager or coworkers.

- *Create pockets of uninterrupted time.* Since interruptions can hamper creativity, do what you can to create uninterrupted time—especially when working on something that requires creative thought. This may mean coming in early, staying late, working from home, or putting a Do Not Disturb sign on your door. More on this in chapter 41.

- *Avoid time pressure.* As you become more organized, you'll be less susceptible to deadline pressure. In subsequent chapters, we'll discuss ways you can stay more on top of your work. For now, just realize that constantly working under deadline pressure limits your creativity.

- *Learn to collaborate with others.* In any work situation, try to establish a team approach. One plus one really does equal three when it comes to creative solutions.

Nurturing your creative self can make your work more enjoyable, increase your abilities, and add to the bottom line. It is well worth your efforts to make your work as good as it can be.

PART III

Gadgets, Gizmos, and Things with a Plug

· 14 ·
The Paradox of the Laborsaving Office Device

I love history. One thing that continually fascinates me is how inventions and technology influence individual lives. While many inventions have clearly made life better, some have also added to our workload. Take, for example, household technology. A friend once asked me, "Why are people working so hard, even though we have laborsaving devices?" Why, indeed? It seems that laborsaving devices, such as vacuum cleaners and washing machines, were designed to create "servantless" households. Beginning in the nineteenth century, middle-class Americans faced a servant shortage. This was a bigger problem than it might appear; most middle-class households could not maintain even a minimum standard of cleanliness without additional help. Household technology replaced people. One person could now use tools to do work that used to require several people. Because jobs were easier to do, however, standards were also raised. For example, because it was now easier to wash clothing, it was no longer acceptable to wear the same outfit all week long. Even though the task was easier, the higher standard meant that those doing laundry had to do it more often and therefore were working as hard as ever.

A parallel situation exists in the workplace. We have some wonderful tools, such as the personal computer, but like household technology, office technology has done two things: eliminated personnel and increased our standards of what is acceptable. These days, fewer and fewer people have personal secretaries or assistants. People often do their own word processing, for example. Still, technology has meant that we are expected to accomplish the same amount of work—or more—with fewer people to help. For example, since it is now a lot easier to edit, we edit a lot more. I've often chuckled at the predictions that the personal computer would eliminate the need for paper. We all know how it really turned out. If anything, our use of paper has quadrupled in the past two decades, and most of it needs to be filed too.

Another laborsaving device is e-mail. I still remember crowding into a classroom at a summer research conference to learn all about the Internet. Now, I can't imagine my work without it. While this has certainly made many aspects of my work more efficient (for example, making it much easier to communicate with groups of people instanta-neously), it has also added a whole new layer to my job. Now I must dedicate a significant portion of my day to writing and answering e-mail—a task that did not exist for me even ten years ago. I also find that I send more correspondence—sometimes, much much more—than I used to because it is so easy.

My point is that technology is often a mixed blessing. The newest and latest is not always best. While technology can make you more efficient, it can also add to your work-load. When making decisions about how you can increase your efficiency, adding technol-ogy is not always the answer. Some technology is inevitable, but you don't need everything that comes down the pike. You must weigh whether what you are adding will really help or whether it is just so much high-tech clutter. To be your most efficient, you must constantly weigh these factors and be selective about which technology you invite to become part of your life.

· 15 ·
Do You Need a Special Program?

As discussed in chapter 14, rapid changes in technology often pressure us to keep up. For some people, that means always having the newest and fastest technological widget. This principle also applies to computer software. As you try to simplify your working life, I'd like you to consider whether a special program is the answer. Oftentimes, the answer will be no.

Case in point: For some time, my colleagues have been after me to get a program that handles my references. I've written books that have as many as eight hundred references in them. I also use many of the same references in different projects. Cutting and pasting these into new works really isn't all that hard. People tell me that my life would be a lot simpler if I bought this program, yet, at this point, it doesn't seem that my life would be any easier. Yes, sometimes I'm tempted, especially when I have to change the reference style. And I may change my mind in the future. For now, though, it doesn't make sense.

In considering such dilemmas, you need to ask yourself whether a certain software program would really help or whether it just seems cool. I'm embarrassed to tell you of times that I have purchased software, only to let it sit gathering dust because I didn't have time to install and learn it properly. Other times, a nice little program will come along that *does* make a significant difference in how I do my work. The trick is how to figure this out before making the purchase. Here are three things to consider:

- *Does the program do something that you do on a regular basis?* If it does, then it may make sense to invest the time and money in it. If not, you may be able to get by without it.

- *Does the program do something you* need *to do?* We have limited amounts of time in our days. While some tasks are nice, they may not be necessary. Ask yourself whether you really need to do what the program offers. For example, I recently spotted a program that promised to help me catalog my entire library. I have hundreds and hundreds of books, and while it would be nice to have them cataloged, I can't imagine taking the time to do it. So, no, I don't think I'll get that program.

- *Is the program worth the trade-off in time and money?* Even if you have determined that the program does do something that you need to do, and that you do this task on a regular basis, does it do it any faster than you do this task, or is there any other benefit that justifies the trade-off? If not, you can probably do without the program. This rule also goes for upgrades on programs you already own.

To reiterate my earlier point, technology is not always the answer. Learning to make judgments about which items are helpful and which are merely clutter will go a long way toward keeping your office free from debris. You'll save money, as well.

• 16 •
Date Book vs. PDA: You Decide

On my first trip to New York City, I had dinner with some high-powered academics. In coming up with a date for us to get together, they both pulled their personal digital assistants (PDAs) out of their bags. I pulled out my paper date book. One of them said, "Date book?" with horror in her voice. It was as if I had pulled out a stone tablet and chisel to write down my appointment. I thought it was funny and had no desire to join them in the digital revolution.

It was on another trip that I decided to finally get a PDA. I was with a colleague and happened to be standing next to her as she was checking into the hotel. She had learned that the hotel we were staying in offered frequent flyer miles on our airline and was busily reading the clerk her frequent flyer number. She told me I should do the same. Of course, I didn't have mine with me, and I knew that I would need to call it in. As you can guess, I never did. Had I had that information with me, however, I would have been able to take advantage of the offer. That incident decided things for me.

In making the decision about whether to stick with paper and pen or to purchase a PDA, there are several things you can ask yourself:

- *What types of information do you need to have with you most of the time?* Do you need any reference material? Do you need your address and phone list? Do you need your master calendar (listing your personal and professional obligations)? Do you have an easy way to carry this material around with you without a PDA?

- *Are you comfortable with technology?* If you are afraid of technology, you are less likely to use a PDA and more likely to just carry it around. The software on these is easy to use, but if you are fearful, try someone else's before you buy one. Otherwise, plan to spend some time learning.

- *Do you spend most of your day at your desk, or do you roam throughout the day?* As a general guideline, I'd recommend that you get something portable (paper or electronic) if you spend more than 10 percent of your day away from your desk. If you don't, you'll end up writing stuff down on odd bits of paper, risking the chance that they will get lost. You'll also have to call people back to confirm or change appointments that you can't check right then, which wastes your time. In terms of portability, PDAs will give more bang for the buck, but either a PDA or paper planner will work.

I'd offer one caution as you consider your options: don't go with the hybrid. I've seen some people who use a PDA that they keep inside a paper planner. That, in my opinion, is a mistake. When you do this, you lose the portability of a PDA, which is its major advantage. You are also more likely to leave it somewhere, since your planner does not fit nicely into a purse or pocket.

In considering whether to go electronic, you must carefully consider what you would use the PDA for and whether it offers you any advantages. You might decide that you can get by just fine, thank you very much, on paper. But a PDA can be a useful tool. You decide.

· 17 ·
Some Pretty Cool Programs for Your PDA

I'm an administrator for an international organization that helps breastfeeding mothers. We have the reputation for being earth mothers. And we are. Yet a funny thing happened at our last retreat. Despite our low-tech reputation, several of us started comparing programs that we had for our PDAs. It's amazing what you can do with these little gadgets if you stop thinking of them as simply electronic date books. Let me whet your appetite.

First of all, consider the massive amount of reference material that is available for PDAs. As a writer, I find it handy to keep an electronic dictionary. I'm frequently away from my desk, working remotely, and it's wonderful to have a dictionary even if my computer is turned off. And this is just the beginning. There is much more available, including food lists for various diet programs, wine and movie lists, and even pocket spreadsheet programs to help with your finances. Here are some other uses:

- *Inventory lists.* There are some wonderful programs that keep track of products that you need to stock or purchase, items you have loaned out, and even items you've promised to return. Some of these programs are for home use, but you can easily adapt them for the office.

- *Travel information.* There are maps available for your PDA. At this writing, these are still not very practical, but you can store lots of other travel information. I record directions, so I don't have to ask each time I visit. I also include any hotel confirmation numbers, telephone numbers, and locations and even the names of good restaurants in the area. Other helpful tools include calculators for tips and electronic expense reports.

- *Contact information.* When you're on the road, it's nice to have contact information with everyone's extension, so you can leave messages or get in touch some other way.

- *Birthday information.* Birthday information, for home or office, can be entered into the existing software, and this information can be automatically updated yearly.

- *E-mail features.* You can now receive and send e-mail on a PDA. While it is not practical to handle all of your e-mail in this way, you can handle short correspondence, even when away from your computer.

- *Music and pictures.* PDAs can even play music. You can load MP3 files and listen to them with a headset. You can also store color pictures, which can eliminate the need to carry them in your wallet.

This information is pretty basic. As I write this, PDAs are becoming even more sophisticated, with combination cell phones, digital cameras, and PDAs being offered. My point is, even with the basic models, you can probably do much more than you imagined. If you are considering getting one, these new features may be the deciding factor.

· 18 ·

Conquering Cord Clutter

I was looking in an office supply catalog recently, and I couldn't help but notice how nice and neat the desks looked. As I stared at these pictures, it finally occurred to me what was different—there were no cords. How different the picture was from most offices, which are often a mass of tangled cords!

Why is it important to address the mess of cords? Because a mess in one area frequently leads to messes in other areas. This observation is based on the "broken window" theory of behavior. This is an economic theory that states that if one windowpane in a building is broken, people are less likely to take care of the rest of the building. This theory may sound familiar. It was the foundation of New York City Mayor Rudy Guiliani's crime-prevention program. If your office is a mass of cords and plugs, the mess may make you less likely to take care of the rest of your office. So what can you do?

Take a hard look at peripherals. Much of our cord mess comes from all the other things we have plugged into our computers. It's good for all of us to periodically examine whether we need all these things. If you have a peripheral you use only periodically, you may decide to store it elsewhere. However, most items you will probably decide you need.

Consider a docking station or USB hub. To handle lots of cords, one central unit that handles them all can simplify the cord mess on your desk or computer table. It will allow you to attach everything in one place.

Manage cords under the desk. Even with a docking station or USB hub, you will probably still need to address the mass of cords under your desk (unless you cannot see them). While you can't make them completely go away, you can make them look a lot more presentable. Here are some possible tools to help you do this:

- *Tie-down strips.* These handy items are available at most hardware stores and come in a variety of colors. Enterprising law enforcement officers even use them as handcuffs when they have a lot of prisoners to escort to jail (just to give you an idea of how strong they are). The downside is that once you put these on, they will need to be cut off if you want to make a change.

- *Velcro strips.* As the name implies, Velcro strips are small strips of Velcro that can be used over and over again. They come in a variety of colors and can be quite handy, especially if you need to rearrange things frequently.

- *Electrical tape.* A less elegant, but still workable suggestion is to use black electrical tape. The downside is that it also needs to be cut off and can make cords sticky.

With any of these techniques, make sure that you leave the cord for your laptop loose, so you can take it with you and leave the rest of the neatly bound cords behind.

Conquering cord clutter is one simple way that you can improve the appearance of your office. The results will be so great, you'll be inspired to tackle the pile on your desk next.

▪ 19 ▪
Computer Maintenance

If you are like most office workers, your computer is your primary tool. It is in your best interest to maintain your computer, even if the company you work for is more casual about maintenance. Getting a new computer is expensive, and it can take several weeks to set it up the way you like. So be careful with yours, and you'll save time in the long run. Some of this you may do for yourself, or you may have a division within your company that takes care of software and hardware problems. In either case, you should know what you can do to help your computer do its best.

Buy antivirus software and yearly updates. Unfortunately, the world being what it is, you need protection from computer viruses. Be sure to get virus protection software and keep it up-to-date with automatic subscription updates.

Vacuum your keyboard every month or two. Computer keyboards are susceptible to all the junk we drop into them, including food crumbs, dandruff, dead skin, hair, and other debris. Yuck! Air spray cans just move stuff around. You need to vacuum out these particles or flip your keyboard upside down and shake it. This will extend the life of your keyboard. Also be extra careful with anything liquid around your computer.

Clean the grill on the back of your computer. If you have a desktop computer, the grill over the fan can get clogged with dust and dirt. This causes the computer to get too hot and can result in premature failure. Clean the grill every month.

Buy a good UPS. UPS stands for uninterruptible power supply. It will do a better job of protecting your computer against power surges than a power strip. It also will protect you against short-term power outages, which is important since most computers don't like to be turned off improperly.

Don't keep personal stuff on your hard drive. Assume that anything on a company-owned computer is fair game for management to read. This includes personal letters, e-mails, and downloads from Web sites. Internet surfing wastes a tremendous amount of time in the workplace, and employers are increasingly tracking sites that employees visit. Employers have also begun firing people for having inappropriate material (like Internet porn) on their hard drives. Someone I know even witnessed the FBI come to his office, haul away a coworker who was visiting child porn sites, and threaten to remove all computers from the work site. Definitely not worth the risk!

Make sure you have properly licensed software. In other words, don't steal! Intellectual property laws are getting teeth these days, and whole companies or departments are being busted for illegally copying software. Often, disgruntled ex-employees phone in tips, and law enforcement may show up and confiscate all of your computers. This is also definitely not worth the risk.

Keep original disk and serial numbers for all software. You may need this information for recovery after a computer failure or for obtaining reduced-cost upgrades from the software vendors. Keep a hard copy of this information.

For better or for worse, computers are here to stay. Your efficiency on the job may depend on having a computer that is up and running on a moment's notice. Only people whose computers have died can fully comprehend how much there is to lose. When it comes to your computer, safe is better than sorry.

▪ 20 ▪
Back It Up!

Backing up your hard drive is a bit like flossing—a good idea, but hardly anyone does it on a regular basis. That is, people usually don't back up their hard drive until after a computer failure. Don't let this happen to you. If you are not regularly backing up your computer, make this your first change in creating more order in your work environment. In considering how to go about doing this, you have several decisions to make. First, you will need to choose the medium that's most appropriate. Then you will need to decide where you will store the backups. Finally, you will need to decide what files to copy.

Choosing Your Medium

When it comes to copying files, you have several possible choices. There are strengths and weaknesses to each approach.

- *CDs and DVDs.* CDs hold only 600 megabytes, so you can't back up your entire computer with them. However, you can back up all your valuable documents. CDs are cheap, less than ten cents each, and CD writers ubiquitous. DVDs are also possible for backups but are a pain. They are slow and expensive to use if you want to back up an entire disk, since you need several DVDs for each backup.

- *USB external drive.* The most cost-effective solution can be a USB external hard drive. This is a hard disk in a case that connects to your USB port. You can back up your whole system, and you can reuse it, again and again. A USB key (a small key you plug into your USB port) is another good and portable option to back up your important data.

- *Tape drives.* Older systems use tape drives. Tapes have now gotten to be prohibitively expensive. They are about $30 each, and they wear out. They are slow, but you can back up your data overnight.

- *Online archiving.* You could also use an online, Internet-based archive service. This offers the extra protection of being off-site, so if something happens to your office, you will not lose your backups, too.

Where to Store Backups

Another key consideration is where to store your backups. For most people, somewhere away from your computer is a good idea, in the event of fire or theft. If you work in an office, you might also want to take some copies home. You definitely should keep copies at home of files that contain your resume, contact information, and e-mail addresses, and any work you've done on your work computer that does not belong to your employer. Be careful about proprietary or classified information—this shouldn't leave the building.

What Files to Copy

What you copy is up to you. Files that change frequently are good choices. For example, you may choose to copy all of your word processing or e-mail files. As a general rule, you may want to back up your files once a week. Once a day would be better but is probably not realistic for most people. Ask yourself how much you can afford to lose. Also, be sure to back up everything before you travel—especially if you are taking your laptop with you.

Finally, be kind to your friends who are less organized than you. When someone does lose their computer files, and they don't have backups, this is not the time to tell them about backups. Think how you would feel!

PART IV

Stemming the Paper and Electronic Tide

• 21 •
Attacking Your Piles Before Someone Calls the Fire Marshal

I'm not naming names, but someone I know had so much paper piled about that the fire marshal declared his office a fire hazard. Don't let this happen to you! Paper is something that can easily bury you. If you don't deal with it in a timely manner, it can soon cover most of the surfaces in your office. Luckily, you can do something about it.

Establish a Time Frame

Depending on how long it has been since you attacked your piles, the time frame needed to deal with them could be a few hours or a few weeks. You can try doing a little each day. Or you may need to supplement this time, at least temporarily, with nonwork time (in the mornings or on a weekend).

Have What You Need

Before you begin, make sure that you have all the tools you need to handle paper (calendar, stapler, paper clips, tape, razor knife, pens, highlighters, letter opener, and mailing supplies). Assemble these tools near the area where you are working.

Pull Out All Envelopes

Start your work by pulling out any envelopes. Open each of these, even if they look like junk. Put anything that requires action into a pile. Recycle the rest.

Pull Out What You Need to Read

Material you think you need to read can be a large part of your office paper clutter. By pulling it out, you can probably reduce your piles by half. Once you have done this, decide how much you actually do need to read. Information that is out-of-date can be recycled. If you do decide to read it, consider cutting out the article(s) or portions you want and recycling the rest. Your razor knife will be handy for this.

Sort the Remainders

Your piles should be a lot thinner now. Take what's left, and sort through the material by creating different piles. Some general categories could include things to file, things requiring a phone call or visit, information about specific projects, travel information, or material related to organizations you belong to. Limit the number of categories because you'll want to work quickly. After this initial sort, you can deal in more detail with these much smaller piles. Some papers may simply need to be filed. For other papers, you may need to take some action, such as making a phone call. Once you've completed these tasks, you can file, pass on, shred, or recycle the paper. Continue working through these smaller piles until you are done.

Keep Up Your System

Once you have whittled your piles down, you'll need to be proactive to keep them from piling back up again.

- *Process all incoming mail in a timely fashion.* Incoming mail can quickly get out of hand. Train yourself to handle mail quickly. Set a maximum length of time that you will go before dealing with all your mail (such as clear the decks by the end of the day or by the end of the week).

- *Develop a system for filing and tracking.* Sometimes paper piles up because piles serve as a 3-D "to do" list. This is generally not a good idea. Learn to track projects without keeping them in plain sight (see chapter 22).

Cleaning out the piles in your office will make your office a more inviting place to be. You'll spend less time thrashing around, and as an added bonus, you'll no longer be a fire hazard.

• 22 •
Beyond the 3-D "To Do" List

If you have office piles, it might be because they are functioning as your "to do" list. The 3-D "to do" list refers to the practice of leaving things out that require action. The underlying logic is that you won't forget about things you keep tripping over. Sounds like it should work. Alas, there is a problem. Last week's projects get buried under this week's projects. Soon, your office is in chaos—and stuff *still* gets forgotten. I've learned the hard way that 3-D "to do" lists don't work. There is a better way.

Get Things off Your Desk

Start with the assumption that you need to keep your desk relatively clear. You may never get *everything* off your desk for very long. But try to keep your piles to a minimum. Here are some ways to do that.

Have a separate place for each project. If you have projects or specific types of work, you might consider dedicating a file drawer (or part of a drawer) to each one. Everything for that task goes into a specific drawer. I find this helpful because I'm frequently working on several projects at once. For example, I often start research for a book a couple of years before I actually write it. As I gather articles and ideas, I start a hanging file folder. Eventually, the amount of material I collect expands to fill a whole drawer.

Use project bins or folders. A variation on the above approach is to use bins or portfolios for various projects. This can also be helpful for small projects or when you don't have filing space. These files are also portable, which can be a bonus if you travel or work off-site.

Track Projects

Once things are out of sight, it's easy to forget all about them. Your attention is naturally drawn to things in front of you rather than to stuff that is neatly put away. To counter this natural tendency, you need to find a way to track projects—especially those with a specific deadline. Here are a few tracking devices that have helped me. Experiment to see what works best for you.

- *Whiteboard.* When I have committed myself to a project, I write it down with the deadline on my whiteboard. You can use whiteboards to keep track of various projects and their due dates.

- *Desk calendar.* If you work at a desk all day, a desk calendar can help keep you on track. You can also write the next day's "to do" list on your calendar before you leave for the day. This strategy will be less effective if your are frequently away from your desk.

- *PDA.* If you use a PDA, you may find this the best way to track deadlines. You can note deadlines and even set the repeat function for the week (or month) before the deadline to remind you of it.

It is possible to work without piles. You'll be less likely to lose things, and your office will be more presentable. You will also feel more in control of the flow of your work. It's definitely worth the effort.

▪ 23 ▪

Getting It Done:
Don't Miss Your Deadlines!

One thing that amazes me is the casual attitude that some people have toward deadlines. If you have trouble meeting deadlines, learning how to meet them in a timely fashion could have a significant impact on your career. Meeting deadlines will also help stem the tide of paper and e-mail in your office. By learning to deal with projects in a timely way, you keep correspondence and documents—paper and electronic—from piling up in your office.

Deadline Management

Surprise is not pleasant when it comes to deadlines. The deadline is upon you before you know it, and there is not sufficient time to meet it. Unfortunately, this has a negative impact on anyone working with you, as well. Learning to manage projects will benefit many people beyond you. These strategies will help:

- *Break the job into bite-size pieces.* Breaking down the project into smaller components is particularly important if deadlines tend to surprise you. What are units that the job can be broken into?

- *Set mini due dates.* Once you have an idea about all the things you will need to do, work backward from the date that the whole project is due and set mini deadlines for yourself. In terms of writing, for example, having a goal of two chapters a month seems a lot more doable than "writing a book."

- *Post the due date for the entire project where you can see it.* If you tend to lose track of the big picture, a visual reminder can help. It can also help if you are working on several projects at once. Whiteboards and wall calendars are good choices for posting this type of information.

Be Flexible about Order of Completion

Another helpful strategy is to be flexible about the order in which you complete parts of a project. With most jobs, you can work on several different parts at once or work on the components in any order. Start with one of the easy parts first. It will get you started and headed in the right direction. You can also skip around, working on different parts at once. That way, if interest lags, or you're waiting for a piece from someone else, you're still making progress.

Allot Twice as Much Time as You Think You Need

There are always surprises in projects—big projects in particular. It's much better to overestimate than to underestimate how long you will need. Do your best to allow yourself enough time. Don't be afraid to allot twice as much time as you think you'll need.

If You Must Miss a Deadline

Sometimes there are circumstances beyond your control, and you cannot complete your work on time. Other times, you miss deadlines because the project was deceptively large.

If you are going to miss a deadline, let the person who is waiting for your work know. See if you can negotiate a new deadline, and then do your best to meet that one.

People who honor their deadlines are unusual in today's world. If you honor them, you will automatically stand out. People will seek you out for future projects, and you will be treating others with courtesy and respect.

▪ 24 ▪
Deciding What to Keep and What to Dump

One person's trash is another person's treasure. In no place is that truer than an office. Once upon a time, we only had to make decisions about paper. Now we must make similar decisions about electronic mail—and sometimes we've printed these out too.

You may have a hard time making the trash/treasure distinction with your own office clutter. There are few hard-and-fast rules for what to keep and what to dump. Much depends on the type of work you do, how long you need to keep things for your particular field, and the type of documentation that you require.

Things You Should Definitely Keep

There are a few documents that you should keep for future reference:

- *Tax information.* You need to keep your tax forms and any documentation necessary for your taxes for at least five years. Seven would be better. That includes receipts, mileage logs, pay stubs, and any other relevant documentation.

- *Legal information.* Keep indefinitely anything relevant to legal obligations, including contracts, correspondence related to contracts (printed or electronic), articles of incorporation, documentation of patents, copyright, or intellectual property rights, and employment agreements.

- *Other legal documents.* Other legal documents include business licenses, stock certificates, paperwork regarding immigration status, insurance information, a record of bad debts, or similar items. Hold on to these as well.

- *Documentation of work you've done.* I once learned of a colleague who had accepted government money to research a particularly hot topic in child development. He published his findings and went on with his life. Several years later, the government agency that funded him wanted proof that he had not doctored his findings. Much of his original data was long gone and had to be reconstructed. It was a costly and stressful mess. If something like this could happen to you, it might be better to err on the side of keeping more documentation than less.

Questionable Items

Many items you have stored will fall into neither the "must keep" nor the "must dump" category. For items in between, ask yourself the following. Your answers can give you some idea about whether you need to keep the item in question.

- *How hard will it be to replace?* Could you replace the document or item if you had to? If the answer is yes, you may be able to let it go.

- *What's the worst thing that would happen without it?* What would happen if you didn't have this piece of paper (or electronic file)? If the answer involves public shame, or anything involving you in handcuffs, you'd better keep it. If the answer is that you'd suffer mild inconvenience, you might be able to live without it.

- *How tight are you on space?* If you have lots of space, you can be more flexible about what you keep. If space is tight, however, you may need to let certain things go.

Only you can decide what to keep and what to chuck. You have lots of options that will keep the files you use every day functional and fitting easily within your work space.

▪ 25 ▪
Dealing with Stuff You Need to Keep

In the previous chapter, I offered some guidelines to help you thin out your files. Once you have done that, you may still have too much to keep in your office. Here are some strategies to help you make further refinements in the items that you keep.

Save the Piece You Need

Are you hanging on to the whole just because it has a small piece of information you need? For example, do you keep an entire letter when all you need is the address? This is easy to do, but it can lead to a mess. Obviously, you should jot down the address and dump the rest, but you may hang on to the paper out of habit. Using a PDA has enabled me to get rid of lots of this type of paper. In pre-PDA days, my Rolodex often served the same function.

In a variation on this theme, I used to hang on to the whole when I wanted only a quote or two. I'd keep an entire article, or even book, because it had a portion I liked. Finally, I got a blank book, copied all the quotations I wanted, and was able to let go of tons of articles and quite a few books.

Shrink It

You may decide to keep an entire paper document but are looking for a way to preserve it without keeping tons of paper. You can do this by shrinking it. One way to shrink documents is to scan them and save them digitally. You can save hundreds of pages of information in a very compact form. The downside, of course, is the labor needed to scan your files. If you have a lot to do, you may consider getting some help—either from someone on staff or a temporary employee (assuming information is not confidential).

Use Active Storage and Archive the Rest

Just because you have to keep something doesn't mean that you need to keep it in your active storage area, the storage area you use every day. File material you don't use on a regular basis and put it somewhere else. Big companies and even many small ones often have storage for archived files. Find out if you do. If you are on your own, you may consider a different part of your office for archived materials. Even putting things in your less accessible filing drawers (the ones farthest from where you sit or those that are hard to reach) can help.

You can follow a similar strategy with electronic mail. You may want to save all your correspondence. If you keep everything in your e-mail's active storage (in your in-box), it's going to make your daily correspondence more cumbersome. One option is to store your past correspondence in another part of your hard drive or even on a separate disk. Not all programs will let you do this, but some (such as AOL) will. You must use the program to open the file. This keeps your e-mail in-box current, making it easier to address incoming correspondence.

Thinking in a different way about the information you need to keep can allow you to come up with a solution that fits your unique situation. The net result is less time spent searching for what you need—giving you more time all day long.

Filing 101: How to Find It Again

I once worked with someone who was the queen of "the pile" method of filing. Sometimes her system worked, and she was able to produce the document she needed. But, as I'm sure you can guess, she also spent an inordinate amount of time thrashing around. When she did file papers, she would put single sheets in folders and scribble a name on the top. She had lots of these small folders, each under a different name. Information that belonged together could easily be spread through ten different folders. I think you can guess the result.

Even methods that look neater than the above example can be as inefficient. Another woman I knew had files that looked fabulous. They were all color-coded and had neatly typed labels. However, she had similar problems in terms of locating the information she needed.

Having observed many approaches, good and bad, I've found a few strategies that are helpful in putting together a filing system that works.

Remember the primary reason for filing. What I'm going to say will sound obvious, but I'm amazed at how often people forget it. The primary purpose for filing is to enable you to locate the information again. It's not to get material out of the way (although this is nice). It's not to give you some busywork to do. You file information so you can find it again. Keep that in mind as you come up with labels.

In labeling, less is more. When it comes to file labels, less is definitely more. Fewer categories are more effective than many, and the broader and simpler the category, the better. For example, if you deal with a particular company on a regular basis, you might have one folder with everything pertaining to that company inside. You might also think about your job by function. For example, you could file together all the information you collect for business travel, or you could put together all the financial material you handle.

As folders grow unwieldy, split them. Once a file reaches a certain thickness (say, over an inch), you might think about splitting it. You can have individual file folders within hanging files. Or you may need separate hanging files.

Don't forget to alphabetize. Lots of files can be taken care of with alphabetical organization. I keep drawers full of research articles, and I might divide them, generally, by topic, but I'm still dealing with an entire drawer full. In order to find the articles I need, I alphabetize by the last name of the lead author. I can generally find what I want in seconds.

Don't cram things. Save your cuticles. Don't make your file drawers so tight that you are fighting to get things inside. If you are out of room, consider thinning the herd by either getting rid of materials you no longer need or by archiving information that you need only on an irregular basis. Keep your file drawers easy to open and use.

Efficient files will save you time every day. You'll be able to find what you need, waste less time, and spare your cuticles. Definitely a win-win all around.

· 27 ·

What the Well-Dressed Filing
Cabinet Is Wearing

What's inside your drawers? I'm speaking, of course, about your filing cabinet. The inside is more important than the outside because it is the part that makes your filing cabinet work. There are several ways to improve the appearance and functionality of your files.

Use Hanging Folders

I recommend hanging folders. This suggestion may be superfluous, since almost every filing cabinet I see is now set up for hanging folders. Occasionally, however, I do see a cabinet that doesn't have these, and it makes many jobs more difficult. Hanging folders allow you to move your files freely within the drawer. You can remove and insert files easily, and they don't fall over when you remove one. If your cabinet isn't set up for hanging folders, don't despair. With most filing cabinets, you can buy frames that will allow you to use hanging files.

Color Is Fun and Functional

I offer my next suggestion with some caution. The new colored hanging folders can be a nice addition—as long as you don't go overboard. Don't make your color-coding scheme so complex that it is impossible to use. That said, color-coding can be useful if you have two or three broad categories to code by. For example, if you are a program administrator, red could be for all files related to travel, blue for financial, and yellow for personnel.

I generally don't use colored hanging folders to color-code. I just enjoy the colors and mix them all together. There is one exception, however. When I took over as an administrator in a large nonprofit group, I inherited a three-foot-high stack of papers that will eventually go to my successor. After sorting through these (and making liberal use of my recycling bin), I used purple label holders for these files only. All my other label holders are clear. That way, when it is time to pass the torch, it will be easy to distinguish between my files and those of the organization. If you are keeping track of different types of information, this strategy may be helpful for you as well.

Label Clearly

I strongly suggest that you invest in a label maker. Label makers do such a great job, you will never go back to handwritten labels. I also prefer to use clear label holders on my hanging files because they are easier to read.

Arrange Your Files So You Can See Your Labels

To make reading the labels a lot easier, I like to put all my labels for hanging folders on the far right. If I have any standard files in the hanging folders, I have all their labels either in the center or on the left. (You can turn the right-sided folders inside out so you can use these too.) That way, your file folders are not blocking the labels for your hanging folders.

A well-dressed filing cabinet is a pleasure to use. You may even decide to show your files to others. Don't do this too often, however; otherwise people will think that you are strange. (Don't ask how I know that.)

▪ 28 ▪
Tidy Drawers:
Make the Most of This Space

Office drawers are wonderful. They keep the top of your work space clear and add to a general neat appearance. In most offices, however, drawers are as rare as hen's teeth. To make matters worse, drawers are often used poorly and may be stuffed full of odd things that have no other home. Good use of drawer space applies the principle of active storage by keeping the tools you need close at hand. Wherever your drawers are, make sure that you use this prized space to its maximum advantage.

Shallow Desk Drawer

Most desks have a shallow middle drawer. This is ideal for small items such as paper clips, staples, binder clips, sticky notes, notepads, and even a few personal grooming items (lipstick, comb, dental floss, breath mints). You can also keep spare pencils and refills for your pens. Address labels and stamps can go in here too.

To get the most out of this space, you must use a plastic drawer organizer. Fortunately, there are lots of configurations to choose from. Organizers will enable you to keep things neat and help you locate little items that you need at a glance. You may also want to line your drawer with padded shelf liners (available at home stores). These will keep your plastic organizer from sliding every time you open and close your drawer.

Drawer Stacks

Most desks have either one or two sets of drawer stacks. The drawer on top is about six inches high and runs the depth of the desk. The bottom drawer is generally large enough for hanging files.

The top drawer is generally perfect for letter-size envelopes. Often this drawer has dividers that work well to keep envelopes upright. The middle section of this drawer can hold deeper items, such as your label maker. I keep an organizer in this drawer that houses the self-inking stamps I frequently use (for example, to endorse checks), my Dictaphone, bookmarks, and unsharpened pencils. These items are too tall for my shallow desk drawer but would get lost in a deeper drawer.

Desk File Drawer

This drawer is ideal for keeping information you must refer to frequently. I keep files for current projects in this drawer. I also have hanging folders for each month. When I receive something I need to do within a certain time frame, or when I accept a speaking engagement for a certain month, I place the file in the appropriate hanging folder.

Filing Cabinets

In chapter 27 I described what to put inside your file drawers. Now, I want to talk about location. Your files don't have to be pristinely up-to-date, as long as you can find what you need. I like to use drawers that are nearest my computer table for current big projects (like books). The drawers that are farther away I use for either future or past projects, where I need to hang on to information but don't necessarily have to refer to it often. Consider having the information you need on a regular basis within easy reach—even if it means moving furniture around.

Well-used drawers can help you locate what you need in a hurry. Make sure you use this space optimally.

· 29 ·
Money Matters: Handling Financial Papers

I once heard a wonderful story about Albert Einstein. When he first came to the United States, he was eagerly hired by an American university. An administrator met with him and inquired about the salary this great scientist required. Einstein is reported to have said that he had considered the matter of his salary and had decided that he could not live on less than $33 a month (or a similar low figure). At this point, the official asked to speak to his wife.

In the course of my career, I've had the chance to work with some truly great minds, and many of these individuals were not wise in the ways of money. Still, lack of wisdom in this area is ultimately not in your best interest. Below are some basics that you need to pay attention to, even if finances are not the central focus of your job.

Tax Information

All of us have work-related expenses that may be tax deductible. It's amazing how often we fail to take advantage of these legal ways to lower our taxes. When in doubt, keep the receipt, and check with your tax person. Here are a few expenses that might be deductible:

- *Business-related expenses.* Keep track of any information or tools you purchased that are relevant to your work.

- *Unreimbursed travel expenses.* In almost any travel, you may have expenses that were not covered. Keep track of these.

- *Professional education.* Any education that you pursue to update or keep your skills current may be deductible. This can also include travel expenses involved in getting to the training.

- *Mileage log.* Keep track of miles you travel for work (beyond your daily commute), for charitable activities, or for medical reasons. All may be tax deductible.

Expenses

I'll admit that I hate filling out expense reports. These can be worth hundreds of dollars, so you need to find a way to turn these reports around in a timely fashion. If your expense report is for a trip, consider completing it before you get home. Once you have returned to your office, thousands of other things may require your attention. It's easy for expense reports to get lost in the shuffle.

Accounts Payable/Accounts Receivable

If you are in business for yourself, it goes without saying that you need to keep track of what you owe and what others owe you. Otherwise, you will not be in business for long. Keeping track is important for the rest of us as well. If doing so is difficult, hiring some help is a good idea. But you should still try to understand as much as you can. Keeping track of this information can be more of a problem for people who do outside work in addition to their regular jobs.

The story of Einstein illustrates that you can be a very smart person but still not be smart about money. Keeping on top of financial details can help you in many ways, and you'll be able to keep more of your money too.

▪ 30 ▪
Set Up a Space for Recycling

Ever since I was a kid, I have hated waste. Unfortunately, offices can waste a lot. The good news is that it is easier than ever to recycle materials. Companies are realizing that recycling is good for their bottom line, as well. If the company is large, the amount saved can be in the tens of thousands of dollars. As you contemplate cleaning and tidying your office, recycling will be important because you will be generating a lot of material that needs to be recycled.

Your office may already be set up to handle your excess. In that case, all you'll need to do is make sure your overflow ends up in the proper receptacle. More challenging is what to do if your office is not set up for recycling. Even then, there are things you can do. If you work in a large company, consider speaking with your manager or human resources department about how to set up a recycling program. The managers may be willing to do it but just haven't gotten around to it yet. Show them how recycling will benefit the company. They may need to know this before they do something that can, at least initially, cost extra money. If you are working with a smaller company, or if you are the only one who wants to recycle, you may need to take a different tack and take care of the recycling yourself. Here are some ways to start.

Decide what you want to recycle. Paper is the most obvious thing to recycle. You can also recycle toner and inkjet cartridges, soda cans, books, computers, and even office equipment.

Find a place that will take what you collect. You may need to take materials home to include with your home recyclables, but this can be a pain. It's better to find someone who will collect recyclables on-site. Many places will take printer cartridges, including some retailers. Ask around before you start to gather materials.

Set up a place to collect recyclables. Designate a place in your office to collect the things you want to recycle. A lot of offices provide employees with blue trash cans for recycled papers. These can be purchased at office supply stores. You might also place recycling bins, for collecting soda cans and bottles or printer cartridges, in places where people congregate. Whatever you decide to do, make it easy for people to participate, or they will be unlikely to do it long-term.

Even little steps help. Even if you are the only one in your office who recycles, every little bit helps. The average person uses 660 pounds of paper every year. If you recycle most of what comes your way, your efforts will mean that 660 fewer pounds of paper end up in landfills. And that's a good thing.

Your recycling efforts can have a significant impact on the environment. I once read of an employee in a large hotel chain. He had decided to quit his job because he wanted to do something that would make a difference for the environment. His company invited him to stay and set up a recycling program for them. His efforts led to chainwide recycling, saving the company big bucks and keeping tons of waste out of landfills. Start small, and there is no telling how far you can go.

· 31 ·

Get E-mail Out of Your In-Box

I was at a conference this past year, and several of us started talking about e-mail. These women were organized and competent but were really getting buried. One woman confessed that she had about five thousand messages in her in-box. Another confessed that she had over eight thousand. Judging from the chagrined looks I saw around the room, these women were not alone. You may not have quite that many, but most people I know feel that they are not as on top of their e-mail as they would like to be. If e-mail is an important part of your work, it is in your best interest to get a handle on it.

Consider Your Internet Provider

One key to e-mail management is keeping your in-box current. In-boxes vary based on your Internet provider. With providers such as America Online, Hotmail, Earthlink, Juno, and Yahoo, all files go into a single in-box. A single in-box can work well, or it may be too limited. In contrast, professional e-mail programs, such as Outlook and Eudora, allow you to use multiple in-boxes. They have other advantages. They are integrated with calendars and PIM (personal information management) tools and can be used with Word and other Microsoft programs, such as Excel, Access, and PowerPoint.

Single vs. Multiple In-Boxes

If you have a high volume of e-mail, you might consider one of the professional e-mail programs so that you can make use of several in-boxes. Senders you need to answer promptly can go into one. If you have more than one account, you can ask this program to check your other accounts as well. You can also create different account names for different purposes (such as business and personal, or public vs. private). Outlook and similar e-mail programs will also save incoming and outgoing mail—indefinitely, if you so desire. One drawback of multiple in-boxes is that it's very easy to let e-mail in less used in-boxes languish. Be sure to watch for this so that it doesn't happen to you.

If you are unsure, the best approach may be to experiment and see what works best. For me, multiple e-mail addresses, or even in-boxes, are not a good strategy because it's too easy for me to ignore messages. I have a single in-box that I try to keep current. When I have read or answered a message, I file or delete it. I always copy the original message into my response, so I have a copy of both message and response.

Decide on a Reasonable Schedule for Answering E-mail

Sometimes when I'm on the road or racing for a deadline, I may choose to ignore e-mail for a few days, but I try not to go longer than a week. Generally speaking, I try to answer urgent e-mail messages by the end of each day, and to empty my in-box by the end of the week. You need to decide what is best for you. And remember, just because e-mail is instant doesn't mean that your response always needs to be.

▪ 32 ▪
Some Shortcuts on Correspondence

A few years ago, we held a ceremony to honor the scholarly contributions of one of my colleagues. Presenter after presenter stood to speak of how this man had contributed to their work in a positive way. In the course of this discussion, something else emerged— his correspondence style. Several people talked about letters that they had written to him, and how he had responded with a handwritten note on the bottom of the original letter. In so doing, he had found a way to answer people in a timely manner. While not elegant, this method was very efficient.

Correspondence can take up an inordinate amount of time in our work lives. While you might not feel comfortable using my colleague's method, you can probably find other ways to save time in your electronic and paper correspondence.

E-Mail Shortcuts

E-mail is a fact of life in most businesses these days. Many of the jobs I do, I could not do without e-mail. On the other hand, it can also be a substantial time hog. Here are some methods to make the process quicker.

Copy the original correspondence. When you receive an e-mail from someone, send their original correspondence in your reply. The recipient will know right away what your reply is in reference to, and you will have a copy after you discard the original correspondence.

Use a different color to answer long e-mail messages. When you have a long or multipart message to answer, using a different color allows you to respond directly to different parts of the message, inserting your answers into the relevant sections.

Use a signature. Take advantage of your e-mail's ability to "sign" your correspondence with your name, address, and other pertinent information. If this information is automatically included in your correspondence, there is less typing for you to do.

Paper Shortcuts

Even with e-mail, paper correspondence is omnipresent. Fortunately, there are ways to speed up this process as well.

Automatize. If there are certain types of correspondence that you do on a regular basis, automatize as much as you can. For example, with our health insurance, I need to submit regular claims. In order to speed up the process, I printed a sheet of stickers with our policy number on them and another sheet with the company address. Submitting claims now takes seconds, rather than minutes. Because it is easy, I'm more likely to keep up with it.

Use postcards. One more old-fashioned tool that can also come in handy is the prestamped postcard. This is especially useful if you need to send a quick response and are either away from your office or don't have access to e-mail. You might also find prestamped postcards handy to send along with a letter that requires a response. Enclose a self-addressed postcard with your question on it. Then all the person needs to do is make the appropriate response and drop the card in the mail.

Finding ways to make your correspondence easier will allow you to keep in touch with others while using your time more efficiently. Just remember, it doesn't have to be pretty to work well.

▪ 33 ▪
My Favorite Things:
Really Cool Office Supplies

One of the advantages of visiting lots of different offices is that I get to see a variety of office products in use. It's made me aware of items that are really handy. Below are a few of my favorites. Some of these you may be familiar with. Others I may be telling you about for the first time. In any event, you may find that these items can help you do your work more efficiently.

- *Sortkwik*. This is one of my favorite products, and I'm amazed at how few people seem to know about it. Sortkwik is the substitute for licking your fingers when handling a lot of paper. It's definitely more hygienic, and it works better too.

- *Double-sided tape*. If you have items on your desk or work area that tend to wander, heavy-duty double-sided tape is useful. I use it on the base of my telephone headset, my business card holder, and other items that tend to get knocked over or out of place.

- *Labeler*. I don't know how I ever survived without this fabulous tool. It is one of the few gadgets that I will suggest you buy. It allows you to make labels for everything, from your files to your file cabinets to your bookshelves. The results are so spectacular, you'll wonder how you ever lived without it.

- *Data flags*. If you need to mark things in a book or article, data flags are another useful item. They work like sticky notes but are smaller and therefore less wasteful. These are even available built into a highlighter. Since you can write on them, I've also found them to be useful as dividers, especially at conferences, when there's a large program book. You can even color-code your program by day.

- *Sharpies.* These fabulous indelible ink markers will write on anything. The small versions of these pens write concisely and neatly. The larger versions will cover anything. They are useful in your mailing area, especially if you are recycling mailing materials and need to cross out information already on the mailer.

- *Telephone headset.* Telephone headsets used to be pretty pricey, but now they're much cheaper. They are useful when you are on the phone but need both of your hands free. I finally bought one after a four-hour conference call. I had spent the last two hours of the call with my neck kinked sideways holding my phone and paid for it afterward. I bought a headset the next day.

- *Desk blotter.* If you want to have some personal items around but don't have room for a lot of frames and other objects, a desk blotter can be a nice compromise. Some come with a plastic sheet that lifts up to enclose pictures. The sheets also provide a smooth surface for writing. I've found them helpful when I need to keep track of little pieces of paper or notes. You'll have a place to keep these scraps safe and also keep your desk clear.

Useful office tools can make your everyday office life more pleasant and even fun. Try out a few of these items and see if you don't find them to be some of your favorite things.

PART V

Managing People and Time

· 34 ·
The Importance of Playing Nice
with the Other Kids

Several years ago, I read about the new CEO of a large biotech firm. She had been out of the paid workforce for several years, while her children were young. Though she had followed a fairly nontraditional career path (at least for her industry), she explained that being a mother of young children had really equipped her for her new job. She conceptualized her role as CEO as needing to help the kids share their toys and play nicely together. It was an astute comment.

Daniel Goleman, in his book *Emotional Intelligence*, made a similar observation. In example after example, he described how technical know-how—what might be considered traditional intelligence—is not enough. Successful people have to have technical ability *and* emotional intelligence—the ability to work with others, to size up interpersonal situations, and understand office hierarchies.

You might wonder what this has to do with being more efficient in your work environment. The answer is that if you can't get along with coworkers, your efforts are likely to blocked at every juncture. One of my husband's friends is a physician. He worked his way through medical school as a nurse. He once commented that nurses could either make it easy or difficult for residents and medical students. Much depended on whether the nurses liked the particular resident or student. They tended not to like the obnoxious ones.

This may seem an obvious point, but I'm amazed at how often it is overlooked. Working in an academic environment, I meet a fair number of colleagues with large egos. Time after time, I've seen people who assume that our office staff should be at their beck and call. I remember one particular woman who was on our staff for less than two days before she managed to totally alienate our office manager. It made her life much more difficult. Bottom line: Treating coworkers and the office staff badly is not only bad behavior, it is D-U-M-B. So here are some suggestions to make your work go more smoothly.

Treat the entire staff with kindness and respect. Remember, every job is important and contributes to the overall effort of your business. If you don't believe me, let your trash stack up for a couple of weeks, and I guarantee that you'll be happy to see the custodial staff.

Get to know your fellow workers. A friend of mine used to work as a secretary in another academic lab. One day, she ran into one of the big honchos, who proceeded to tell her about everything he was involved in, without asking her anything about her life. There's nothing wrong with sharing information about yourself as long as you express interest in others as well.

When you expect extra from your employees, respond in kind. Don't just expect your coworkers or staff to work after-hours, during holidays, or on weekends. Offer something in way of compensation, such as a gift, comp time off, or at least a meal. Realize that they are giving time that they could spend with their families or friends. Recognize their sacrifice on your behalf.

Your staff and coworkers can make a huge difference in how efficient you are. Everyone has an important role to play. If you remember that fact and respond accordingly, your work life will be more pleasant and more productive too.

· 35 ·
Networking vs. Being a Mensch

I might as well tell you: I positively loathe networking. As I sit here, I imagine myself at some networking event, holding a hot hors d'oeuvre, and I'm struck with the strong urge to flee. I have nothing against hot hors d'oeuvres. Quite the contrary. But I often dislike events where they are served. For me, the most distasteful aspect of networking is being nice to people solely to get something from them. Yuck!

Does this mean I've stalled my career? Not at all. I've simply found another way. I resolved, early in my career, that I wanted people to know me by my work, not by my witty repartee at some overcrowded party. (And believe me, academics can throw some really deadly parties!) My way was to focus on being a mensch. *Mensch* is a wonderful word derived from Yiddish that translates into "a real human being." It is someone who combines kindness, responsibility, and dignity. In chapter 34, I described how your ability to get along with others can increase your efficiency. Consider being a mensch an advanced form of getting along with others.

Share Your Work

Get known in your field by turning out really good work and sharing it with others. One way of getting your work known is to send it to people who are doing similar work. You can say something like, "I really enjoyed your presentation/article on such-and-such topic. You might be interested to know about my work in a similar area." If you are shy, e-mail can work well in this capacity. A few people may react badly. But for the most part, people appreciate it. Junior colleagues are now sending me their work, and I always enjoy receiving it.

Do Some Volunteer Work

Volunteer work can also lead to interesting opportunities. I've made some great connections while also giving to others. For example, I served on a committee once that put me in contact with the leadership of a large organization. I didn't try to network in the traditional sense, yet the contacts I made eventually led to two book contracts and several other opportunities.

Do Something Helpful

You don't need to go overboard with this, but being helpful can be another useful strategy. If you see an article someone you know might like, for example, send it to them. I remember once running across an article that I knew a colleague in another state would be interested in. I ran off two copies instead of one and popped the second one in the mail. She really appreciated it, and two years later, she invited me to speak at her campus.

Say Thanks

When someone does something nice for you, take a few minutes and write a note expressing your gratitude. E-mail is acceptable to thank people for small niceties. For something more significant, a written note or maybe a small gift is appropriate. Your actions indicate that you are not taking others for granted. Everyone likes to be acknowledged.

Contact with others in your field can really help your career. Approach these opportunities with the attitude that you are there to be helpful, rather than to get something. You will stand out, and hopefully, you won't have to attend any networking events.

· 36 ·
Dealing with Two-Legged Interruptions

In any office, you are likely to mix with all sorts of people. Some will, unfortunately, be pretty good at keeping you from getting your work done. While it is wonderful to have work friends, you need to set some limits on when and how much you interact. Here are some strategies to try with someone who is interrupting your work.

Talk to the Person

This is the most straightforward of your options. Just say something like this: "I'm glad you stopped by, but now I have to get back to work. I have to turn this in at four." If it is a social visit and you want to chat further, set a time to meet for lunch or a break. You don't need to be rude, but you need to remember that you are there to work.

Use Nonverbal Cues

You might also find that nonverbal cues can let people know that it is not a good time to chat. As I describe in chapter 37, how you position your desk will make it easy or more difficult for people to interrupt you. Beyond how you position your desk, there are a few other nonverbal cues that can give others the hint. For example, when people interrupt your reading, leave your finger on the place where you have just left off. That will let them know that you have a task to return to. This may be too subtle for some, however.

Turning back to your work can also give someone a hint that they need to go. You might also try wearing headphones when you need to concentrate. This may not always work, however. I once shared an office with a woman who viewed all office mates as her full-time counselors. While it is nice to be sympathetic, at a certain point you have to stop. I tried everything I could think of. Once, as I was wearing headphones and looking down at my reading, she actually laid across my desk to get my attention (I'm not making this up). I eventually had to move to a different office.

Close Your Door

This is the ultimate nonverbal cue. But even this may not deter some from wanting to talk with you. Plus, you may not have a door. You might try posting a sign asking people not to disturb you. This strategy will be more effective if you don't abuse it (doing it all day long), and if you let people know when they can come see you (after, say, 2:00 P.M.). Be sure to actually be available then. Alternatively, you can make a specific appointment.

Use Your Mailbox

A substitute for a face-to-face exchange can be for coworkers to leave something in your mailbox that you need to respond to or review. I remember once when my boss was out of town, and I had to work directly with our section chief. Over the course of an afternoon, we blasted out a huge amount of work, and we did it via our mailboxes. She'd work on a section and then leave it for me. I'd pick it up, work on my part, and pass it back. (We did it with hard copies, but this could also be done with e-mail.) Later, she commented on how much she had enjoyed working with me and was amazed at how much we accomplished. We were probably so productive because we weren't interrupting each other and could focus on the task at hand.

In summary, there are ways that you can let people know you need to get work done. You can be firm without being rude, and set a clear boundary between work and social time.

• 37 •

Feng Shui in the Office: How Desk Placement Can Limit Interruptions

There used to be a funny television commercial in which family members were moving furniture in an old woman's bedroom. Depending on where the chest of drawers was located, she either sat up or collapsed. It was an advertisement for a health Web site, and the actions of the actors were in reference to an article entitled, "Feng shui, Does It Really Work?"

Feng shui is the ancient Chinese art that addresses how environments can influence our health and well-being. Here in the West, we've suddenly become interested in this ancient art. It's making us aware of our environments in ways we haven't been before.

What you may not realize is that for a long time psychologists in the West have also been studying the effects of our environment on us. A great deal of research goes into the placement of items on store shelves or of booths in restaurants. For example, in restaurants, have you ever noticed that you feel more comfortable seated along the wall than you do seated in the middle of the room? Furniture style and placement can influence how long you linger in a restaurant or other public space.

Smart furniture placement can also help you become more efficient at work. How you place your furniture can influence how long others linger in your office or whether they feel comfortable interrupting you. Before you start moving your desk, however, you must first consider the characteristics of your job.

Does Your Job Require Interruptions?

In certain situations, it is part of your job to be interrupted. For example, many employees, from receptionists to sales clerks to on-call physicians, are, by definition, interruptible.

People in these types of occupations cannot control when others will need them. If you have this type of job, you need to be accessible. Along these same lines, if you are managing a group of people, they may need to pop in to ask questions or talk to you from time to time.

Can You Be Less Accessible?

You may not need to be fully accessible. Once you have considered the amount of accessibility you want to communicate, here are some options for desk placement:

- *Facing your door or opening.* This is the most accessible position for your desk. It is easy for people to make eye contact with you. It is also the position where you are most subject to the distraction of people walking by.

- *Your back to your door or opening.* This is the least accessible position. People walking by won't distract you, but you also won't see who needs you. People will need to walk into your office to get your attention, which can really break your concentration.

- *Diagonal or sideways placement.* This position, where you are facing the corner opposite your door or are sideways in relation to your door, allows you to be accessible without necessarily being distracted by people walking by. This may be the best general-purpose position for your desk.

How you place your desk can make you more or less accessible, depending on the needs of your job and your ability to concentrate. In the next chapter, I'll describe some similar strategies for your other office furniture that will help you get more done.

▪ 38 ▪
Placing Office Furniture and Tools to Increase Your Efficiency

In chapter 37, I described how desk placement can increase your efficiency by placing limits on your accessibility. The placement of other furniture and tools can also support your efforts to work efficiently. Some of these next considerations are not related to interruptions. Rather, they have to do with actions that may break the flow of your work.

Extra seating. In considering office interruptions, you might give some serious thought to how much extra seating you want in your office. You don't want to make your office so comfortable that others just come and hang out when you have work to do. On the other hand, if you have regular meetings in your office, you will obviously need some extra seating. You might experiment with where you place your extra chairs so that they encourage work but don't encourage people to just hang out.

Computer placement. If you have your computer on your desk, make sure that you are not facing a window. Facing a window forces your eyes to make constant adjustments between the outside light and the glow from your screen. This can cause eyestrain. Even if you are not directly next to the window, pay attention to glare. You may need to move your computer or put up a shade.

Other worktables. If you have another worktable (such as a computer table), make sure that it is the right height for you to work comfortably and that it's close to your desk, so it is easy to move between the two.

Reference materials. If you have any reference materials that you regularly use, make sure that they are near your computer or telephone (depending on where you use them). You are more likely to use them if they are within easy reach.

Files you use most frequently. As I described earlier, use the principle of active storage to keep files you refer to frequently near you. This may mean keeping some files in your desk drawer rather than your filing cabinet. I find that if my files are handy, I am much more likely to refile items right after I'm finished with them.

When I'm working on a specific project, I keep all the materials I need for that project in the drawer nearest my computer table. When I've completed that particular project, I may move the files, or actually the entire drawer, to another spot and bring the materials I need for the next project closer to my table.

By giving thought to where you keep things in your office, you can make your day flow more easily. This will mean less wear and tear on you and less stress by day's end.

▪ 39 ▪

Dealing with Conflicting Priorities

I once had a job where the entire staff hated Monday mornings. Aside from the normal reasons to hate Mondays, we all hated them because one of the senior researchers would spend the entire weekend thinking of things she wanted us to do. She would come in and bark orders at the staff (whom she sensitively referred to as "dweebs"). It didn't matter that most of us did not work for her or that the work she wanted us to do conflicted, in terms of timeline and priority, with tasks that our actual bosses had asked us to do. We got in the habit of hiding.

One of the most challenging aspects of working with others is when you have conflicting priorities. It can be very difficult if you have more than one boss—each of whom may give you assignments and each of whom may assume that their job is the top priority. This can also happen if you work for only one person, especially if that person changes his or her mind frequently about what you should be working on. This type of shifting back and forth between projects can make you less efficient. You may also feel highly stressed by the end of the day because it feels like you never get anything done. Learning some strategies to deal with conflicting priorities can make you feel more in control of your workday.

Track Your Communications about Priorities

If you keep a list of your projects and their due dates, you can tell the person who wants to give you a new assignment that you have these other priorities. If it's your boss, you can then respectfully ask which of these projects should be put on hold in order to meet a new deadline. Communicate that you are not trying to get out of work but that you are merely trying to meet deadlines that you have already agreed to. If you have multiple bosses, ask them to contact the boss who gave you the assignments you already have on your task list, to ask if you can be released from one task so you can work on the other. Be sure to jot down notes summarizing your conversation about the change in priorities. That way, if someone wants to know why the original project is not yet complete, you've documented the change in priorities.

Look Busy

If you are at work and you look bored, you may find yourself tapped for extra projects. If you work at a reasonable pace and look like you are working (as opposed to staring into space), people are less likely to come up with extra projects for you to do.

Be Willing to Help in a Pinch

Sometimes, if there is an emergency, you may need to pitch in and help. Where this gets to be a problem is when there is *always* an emergency. A woman I know never finishes her projects until the last possible minute; she then expects her staff to stay late or work all weekend. She assumes that this is fine, but her high level of staff turnover says otherwise.

Conflicting priorities can be a challenge, but it's one you can generally work out. By respectfully pointing out other agreed-upon priorities, you can be more proactive about the flow of your work. In extreme cases, however, you may need to change jobs. Hopefully, this will be a last resort. If all else fails, you can always try hiding!

· 40 ·

Reach Out and Touch Someone: Telephone, Friend or Foe?

The telephone is a wonderful invention. It allows us to be in touch with people who live far away or call for assistance in an emergency. I would hate to be without one. Like many modern inventions, however, the telephone has a dark side that can make us less efficient on the job. Fortunately, there are some ways to tame the telephone's dark side and make it less likely to become a major source of stress.

Don't Be Available 24/7

Set limits. This suggestion goes for either your office or home phone, but most definitely for your cell phone. Somehow, we've gotten to the place where we think that just because we *can* be available, no matter where we are and what we are doing, that we *should* be. How often have you been with someone and had your conversation interrupted by a chirping cell phone?

If you are going to tame your phones, you must first make a conscious decision about when you need to be available and when you don't. You may leave your phones on without much thought. If you are going to get a grasp on your schedule, however, you must be unavailable for some period of time every day. Here are some candidates for when the phone should be off.

- *When you need to concentrate.* If you are working on something that requires concentration, your chance of making mistakes is drastically increased if you are interrupted. It will also take you longer than the mere length of the phone call to get back to where you were.

- *When you are in a meeting.* Generally speaking, when you are in a face-to-face meeting with someone, you should be fully present. To do otherwise is rude and wastes the other person's time, and yours. The one exception is when you've been trying to reach someone and they finally call back. In that case, I would explain ahead of time that I might have to take a call and give the person I'm meeting with the option of staying or returning to his or her desk if the call comes in.

- *When you are with your family or friends.* Everyone deserves to have some nonwork time during the week. When you sit down to have dinner, with rare exceptions, you should let your machine or voice mail pick up your calls. Similarly, having a cell phone allows you to be out and about, not sitting around waiting for a phone call, but that doesn't mean you should be available for every call. Be selective about when you have your telephone turned on. Obviously, this doesn't apply to doctors on call, but we are not all doctors on call—and even doctors have days off.

Your telephone can make your life easy or difficult. By choosing not to be available 24/7, you take back some control of your life. This will help lower your stress level, make you more efficient on the job, and improve your key relationships. Really, how can you lose?

• 41 •
Calm in the Midst of the Storm: Creating Pockets of Do-Not-Disturb Time

Finding uninterrupted time in a busy office can be a major challenge. If you are doing anything that requires concentration, however, uninterrupted time is a must. The task before you remains how to balance legitimate interruptions with time you can use to concentrate.

Have Daily Office Quiet Time

I first observed this technique in the household of a large family. The mother was one of the most laid-back caregivers I had ever seen. One technique she employed was a daily hour of quiet time. Her older children did not have to nap, but they needed to play quietly in their rooms for that length of time. It helped calm everyone's nerves and gave the mother some much-needed downtime.

You may be able to persuade your coworkers or boss to cooperate if you can convince them that they too will have some quiet time to concentrate. However, this technique requires everyone's cooperation, and you may have coworkers who feel that you or they need to be accessible all day.

Make Good Use of Voice Mail

There is nothing wrong with using your voice mail when you are trying to concentrate. Generally speaking, it is not efficient for you to always be available. Just be sure to return calls in a timely fashion, perhaps by the end of the day. The same is true for e-mail. Checking it once or twice (if you must) a day is generally sufficient. It is perfectly reasonable to let e-mail sit for a couple of hours or even days when you need time to concentrate. It lowers your stress level too.

Work Different Hours

You may need to come in early or stay late to get uninterrupted time. Unfortunately, you may end up working additional hours. This is not a great strategy if it becomes a regular feature of your job, but it can work well when you have a key deadline.

Go Off-Site

If you need an extended period of quiet, you may need to vanish for a while. This may mean working from home. It may mean packing your supplies and heading for the library, a conference room (particularly if it's on a different floor), or even your local coffee shop.

You can take control of your work life and create pockets of uninterrupted time, even in a busy office. These quiet periods really can become the calm in the midst of the storm and will benefit everyone in the office.

· 42 ·
"I Can't Hear You": Controlling Noise

In most offices, a drone of noise is constantly in the background. Stop and listen to what you can hear. You're likely to notice other people's telephone conversations, coworkers chatting outside your door, the radio in the next cubicle, outside traffic, and the whir of office machinery. Researchers are finally recognizing what most of us have known for a long time: office noise can be a significant source of stress. It can also impair your ability to concentrate, meaning that every job takes longer. Controlling noise can help you be more productive and less stressed on the job. Fortunately, there are several positive steps you can take.

Determine Your Optimum Level of Noise

Try to get a sense of how much background noise is good for you and what level makes it difficult to concentrate. We are all different. Some people need total silence in order to concentrate. You may (like me) do better with some background noise as long as it's not directed toward you (people actually talking to you). I once had a temporary job where I had to sit in a white room all day sorting things by zip code. There was no background noise, and I spent the day staring at blank walls. By the end of the first day, I was suffering from total sensory deprivation. I brought a radio in the next day.

You may also find that sometimes having some background noise helps while at other times it is distracting. Try to match the task before you with an optimum level of noise.

Control the Noise around You

You have several options to make your work space more livable in terms of noise.

- *Create your own background noise.* If you are creating noise to drown out unwanted noise, the noise level will feel more within your control and the noise itself will be less stressful. Some examples are playing background music, using a white-noise machine, or a using a desktop fountain (although you may have a sudden urge to run to the bathroom). Make sure your background noise is not distracting to others.

- *Use headphones.* This is not a practical option if you need to answer the phone many times a day. However, if you are working on something steadily and letting your voice mail pick up your phone, headphones can work well. Newer models even have sound-muting capabilities to drown out background noise. Headphones are also a great nonverbal signal to would-be interrupters.

- *Try working alternate hours.* If noise is too bad, or you need an extended quiet period, you can also try coming in earlier or staying later. Even if you only do this for an hour at a time, you can often accomplish a significant amount of work.

Finding a way to control office noise can leave you feeling refreshed rather than frazzled at the end of the day. Even in a shared office there are ways that you can get some control over this common source of office stress.

· 43 ·
Some Thoughts on Multitasking

Multitasking. It's that important art of doing two or more things at once. It seems that multitasking is everywhere these days. We talk on the phone on our way to work. We read while we exercise. We put on makeup as we drive (generally, not a good idea!). We type while we are on the phone. Even our computers are doing it. And no doubt about it, multitasking can make us more efficient. It allows us to use time that would otherwise be wasted, such as when we are on hold or standing in line.

As good as it is, however, multitasking is not all sunshine and song. As with any tool or technique, it can be used to your advantage or it can be abused. In this chapter, I offer some observations on multitasking to help you use it to your advantage.

Don't Assume It Is Better to Do More

In our culture, we labor under the illusion that more is better. Not necessarily! Sometimes doing more than one thing is not only less efficient, it is downright dangerous. For example, many states now ban talking on the phone while driving. Even the hands-free models can be a serious distraction for drivers. Here are some times when it is good to focus on only one thing:

- *When you need to concentrate.* If you are trying to complete a complicated form, write, or do any kind of accounting, it's best to focus on only that task.

- *When you are talking with someone.* Although lots of people do it, it's rude to talk with someone while you are also using your computer. On occasion, you can do something brainless, like dust or sort through junk in a drawer, without impairing your ability to communicate. Sometimes we try to do more than that, though, and our actions communicate disrespect (even if unintentionally) to the person we are conversing with.

- *When your life depends on it.* Some situations require concentration if you want to be safe. Driving is one example. Using something sharp or mixing something that could be poisonous are other examples. Even something that's critical to your work life, like working on a key document, requires your concentration.

Try Living in the Present

One of the real downsides to multitasking, in my view, is that it keeps us from being fully present. From time to time, it is okay to multitask. Sometimes, though, it becomes a way of life. You are never fully engaged with any task but are thinking about the two or three other things that you are also doing.

Not surprisingly, multitasking as a way of life can have a dramatic impact on your stress level and even your health. For example, how often do behaviorally oriented weight-loss programs tell participants to concentrate when they eat and to avoid eating when they are also walking, watching TV, or reading? I might add driving a car. Take a few minutes to actually taste your food. Otherwise, it's very easy to overeat. Similarly, it's important to pay attention when you drive. Otherwise, you can be putting yourself and others in danger.

Multitasking has its place. Learn to be conscious about when and how you apply it. Be sure to spend some time every day living in the present. In the long run, you'll be less stressed, make fewer mistakes, and probably get more done too.

· 44 ·
Identify Hidden Time Wasters

As I described in the introduction, Americans are working longer hours than ever. We've also found more ways than ever to waste time while at work. If you are feeling overwhelmed by the amount of work that you have to do, you might consider whether hidden time wasters have slipped into your day. If you become aware of ways that you whittle your day away unproductively, you'll have the opportunity to eliminate these time wasters and work smarter not harder. Here are some common ways that all of us can waste time at work.

Gathering around the Water Cooler

This one is so common, it's even part of our lexicon. Getting to know your coworkers is a legitimate part of work, but doing it habitually gobbles up tons of time. Honestly, do you really need to discuss last night's episode of *Survivor* (or another hot show)? Do you really need to talk about what a doofus your boss is—again? Or to hear someone else's similar tale? Are those conversations really worth being away from home because you have to work late to catch up on everything? Try to limit these conversations to a few minutes, or have them at lunch.

Personal Counseling

Do you have coworkers whose lives are in perpetual crisis, who behave in self-destructive ways, or who require that coworkers or employees perform as their support network? I'm not talking about someone who is facing a discrete crisis. I've seen some wonderful examples over the years of coworkers rallying behind someone who is battling cancer, or whose spouse has died suddenly, or who is recovering from a terrible automobile accident. I'm talking about the person who is always wallowing in problems. By providing emotional support, you may actually be supporting this dysfunctional behavior. It is, most decidedly, *not* your job to constantly help someone who will take no steps to help himself or herself. If you still want to help, try to do it when you are not working.

Cyberslacking

There's a new word in our language: "cyberslacking." Cyberslacking refers to wasting time by surfing the World Wide Web. Companies are realizing that cyberslacking costs them billions each year in lost productivity, and they are beginning to crack down. Most companies turn a blind eye if this privilege is not abused. So a few brief minutes of looking up something isn't a problem. When those minutes become hours, you have a problem.

Computer Games

Computer games, online or otherwise, can also eat up lots of work time. I love computer solitaire, but I had it removed from my computer when I realized how much time I was wasting. I still occasionally play, but on my own time. If you find that computer games take up more than a couple of minutes, save them for your home computer, or consider eliminating them entirely.

By identifying hidden time wasters, you can save minutes, or even hours, each day. That means more time to do things outside of work with people you care about. Isn't that worth it?

PART VI

Away from the Office

· 45 ·

On the Road: The Portable Office

We live in a mobile society, and work often takes us away from our offices. Working remotely can be a challenge for even the most organized worker. Workers who are less organized may find it next to impossible to stay on top of things when on the road. There are, however, some simple things that you can do to be more efficient away from your office.

Create a Portable Office

I first assembled a portable office a few years ago, and it's been quite helpful. I have since made several of these for friends who coveted mine. They like theirs, too.

I start with a small, clear makeup bag (easily purchased at discount department stores). Clear is important so you can see where everything is. Six to eight inches is a good size. Pick this up first, since you will want to make sure that the other items you buy will fit inside. After you have your bag, add scissors ("student" scissors will fit—but don't get the ones with plastic blades), a glue stick, mini stapler and staples, paper clips, binder clips, sticky notes, return address labels, a couple of shipping labels, indelible marker, highlighter, razor knife, tape, correction fluid, a small notepad, postage stamps, and data flags. I also have a small dispenser with packing tape, but I pack this separately.

Since this bag includes a scissors and a razor knife, don't pack it in your carry-on bag if you are flying. Stash it in your suitcase, and check your bag. You will find many uses for your portable office on the road. Be sure to replenish any supplies you use once you come home.

Keep Up with E-mail

I try not to answer e-mail when I'm on vacation, or I do it in a very limited way. When traveling for business, however, it is generally in your best interest to keep up with it. If you deal with urgent messages, you can answer the others in a more leisurely fashion when you get back to your office. If your e-mail has automatic messaging, use it to inform people who send you messages that you are out of the office. That way, they won't be annoyed when you don't get right back to them.

Consider Bringing a Printer

If you are somewhere where you are planning to do a lot of writing, you might consider packing a printer in one of your bags. Don't laugh. I was on the road once and was getting ready to send in a book. I was really grateful that I could print out multiple drafts and edit hard copies. It would have cost me a fortune to do this at a copy center or cyber cafe. I know someone else who ended up buying a printer while on the road. It is now her travel printer. If you do decide to bring a printer, be sure to remove the toner or ink cartridge and wrap it securely in plastic.

While you cannot bring all the comforts of home with you when you travel, you can do some things to ensure that you are your most productive. Then, when you get back to the office, you can take your time acclimating instead of being overwhelmed by the backlog that built up while you were away.

· 46 ·
How to Keep Your Desk from Becoming Buried While You're Gone

I travel a lot in the spring and summer, and sometimes I return to find my desk completely buried. I have just enough time to dig out before it's time to leave again. Still, I have found some strategies that make it easier to return to a more orderly office.

Have Everything Placed in Your In-Box

One of the problems I've had to deal with is piles collecting everywhere. It helps a lot if people put everything in my in-box that comes in when I am away. If nothing else, it leaves the rest of my desk free from debris, so I at least have a place to work.

Sort Third-Class Mail Separately

If I am gone a long time, I may have whoever brings my mail to my desk separate third-class from first-class mail. Third-class mail tends to be bulky, and much of it is junk. If it is in a separate pile, I can go through it at my leisure and take care of the more urgent first-class mail right away.

Get Assistance at Your Office

If possible, you might consider having your assistant, secretary, or coworker go through your mail with you on the phone. There may be things that this person can take care of for you while you are gone. If you don't have an assistant or secretary, consider some type of reciprocal relationship with a colleague.

Check Voice Mail and E-mail Daily

As I mentioned in chapter 45, it's wise to check your e-mail with some regularity while you are gone. If you can't check it every day, try to check it at least every other day. You don't necessarily have to answer it all, but at least take care of the more urgent messages. Waiting in an airport is often a perfect opportunity to answer e-mail that is less urgent. Send it when you get to your next location.

Follow a similar procedure with voice mail. Phone in for your messages at least every other day (every day may be better). Return any calls that are urgent. You can also answer queries by e-mail, or leave answers on voice mail. This can be helpful, especially when you are in a different time zone.

Let Others Know When They Might Expect Your Work

Being on the road can make it challenging to get some projects done. If you find that you are behind schedule and don't have time to finish a project before you go, contact the person who is waiting for work from you and let him or her know when to expect it. Explain that you are traveling but will be able to deliver it in X number of days. Then make that new deadline.

Coming back to the office need not be a nightmare. While away, you can handle some of your tasks remotely and put others on hold. Less pileup on your desk means less stress and headaches for you once you return to your office.

▪ 47 ▪
Travel Safely and in Style

I still remember the first time I ever traveled for business. I was so thrilled. I wanted someone to ask me what I was doing. The luster has, unfortunately, long since worn off, but I've learned a lot about how to travel well. A horrendous travel experience can decrease your efficiency either at your destination or once you return to the office. But, with practice, you can minimize these. Over the years, I've learned a few things that can help make your trip more pleasant and more productive.

Dress Comfortably but Presentably

Even on direct flights, it is possible for airlines to lose your luggage. Therefore, I suggest that you give some thought to what you wear. This doesn't mean you need to wear a suit and uncomfortable shoes (and you probably shouldn't, in case you need to evacuate). But you probably should not wear a sweat suit either. If your luggage was lost, could you wear what you have on to your appointment the next day? If the answer is no, then you might want to ratchet things up a bit. After the first day, you will most likely have an opportunity to buy something, if necessary.

Pack an Emergency Kit

I learned this the hard way. Now I always pack a kit with fresh underwear, toothpaste, toothbrush, shampoo, sewing kit, and my prescription medicines in my carry-on bag. With regard to any medicines that you need, I recommend that you keep them in your carry-on *and* your suitcase.

Bring Food and Water

Airline food has never been great. Now it is often nonexistent. If you've ever had forty-five minutes to catch a connecting flight—at dinner time—than you will recognize the wisdom of this suggestion. I've arrived at my hotel at 9:00 P.M., not having eaten since lunch. Not eating is pretty much guaranteed to make me crabby. Now I always pack protein bars, water, and often some fruit. This can be handy too when it is difficult to find breakfast items where you are staying. Fortunately, protein bars are widely available. I recommend these, rather than granola bars, since granola bars are mostly carbohydrates, and you will be hungry again shortly after eating one.

Watch Out for Your Safety

I've never had any trouble when I've traveled, but I am conscious of my safety and diligent about things that may compromise it. Here are a few suggestions:

- *Don't let hotel front desk staff say your room number out loud.* Most big hotels do a good job; however, I've had some clerks say my room number loudly enough to be heard from across the room. When that happens, I've refused the room, told them to not say the number out loud, and requested another. It's better to be safe than to be best friends with the desk clerk. You can do this politely but firmly. It will, hopefully, protect the next traveler as well.

- *Never wear your name tag outside the hotel.* Nothing shouts "tourist" louder than a conference or meeting name tag. Always take yours off before leaving the hotel.

- *If in doubt, take a cab.* In a city, even in the middle of the day, if you don't know where you are going, take a cab. It is better to be safe than thrifty, even if you have to pay for it yourself.

▪ 48 ▪
What to Do Before You Leave Home

In the last chapter, I described some things you can do to make your business travel safe and comfortable. Here are some suggestions of what to do before you leave so you can make your business travel more pleasant and your work more efficient while away. While you can't plan for every contingency, you may be able to avoid some common problems.

Confirm Your Reservations

Don't leave home without confirming your reservations. I learned this one the hard way when I arrived in a city at 9:30 P.M., only to be told that there was no room at the inn. Now I always call ahead of time. Do this with any rental cars, limo/shuttle service, and flight information as well.

Find Out about Ground Transportation

When calling the hotel to confirm your reservation, ask about ground transportation. The hotel may have a free shuttle from the airport. If it doesn't, it can probably recommend a shuttle service. Knowing this ahead of time can make it much easier to get to your hotel once you arrive and can also save a significant amount of money since you won't have to take a cab.

Leave a Copy of Your Itinerary Behind

Be sure to let people in your office and at home know where you are. Leave an itinerary with someone. This will be helpful if you lose your e-tickets too. Make sure to leave this information with someone who has a fax.

Copy Any Cards You Carry with You

Before you go, photocopy all your credit cards (front and back) and your passport. Leave this information with someone who has a fax. Then, if your purse or briefcase is stolen, you can have your friend or colleague fax this important information to you.

Put Tags and Markers on Your Bags

In case you haven't noticed, suitcases can all look the same. One way that you can prevent someone from grabbing your bag by mistake is to mark yours clearly. Put name tags on all your bags. I've had no luck with hard plastic tags that are available at travel stores, as they tend to shatter when luggage is moved behind the scenes. I've had much better luck with laminating my business cards and attaching them to my bags. These business-card tags are cheap, never break, and they have my business, not home, address on them (important for security reasons). I also attach a short piece of colorful ribbon to my bags. This makes it very easy to recognize your bag (don't make it too long, however, or it might get caught on the conveyor belt).

Ship Some Stuff Ahead

Airlines have lowered the maximum weight you are allowed to take in a suitcase from seventy pounds to fifty pounds. If you need to bring a lot of materials with you when you travel, this can be a problem. I've found it helpful to ship some stuff, such as conference materials, ahead to my hotel. Most hotels also have shipping available if you need to send items home. And if you are in the United States and have access to a car, you might consider the U.S. Postal Service or one of the UPS franchises. Both sell packing materials, in case you've been shopping heavily while gone.

· 49 ·

Make a Smooth Transition
between Home and Office

Home offices are now a part of many people's lives. Some home offices have become places of full-time employment. For others, a home office may be a place to work one or two days a week. As with working remotely, you may find that it is difficult to seamlessly go back and forth between your work office and your home office. Since a lot of information is already available on setting up a home office, I want to focus here on how to merge your home and work offices, so you can work more efficiently.

Your Computer Needs

Computer use is one of the most difficult aspects to coordinate. Unless the work you do at home is really completely separate, you might seriously consider using only one computer that you bring back and forth. Otherwise, you may have a desktop computer in the office and a portable laptop, or you may have a desktop computer at home and another at work. Either of these situations can be challenging since you almost invariably have the wrong version of the file on the computer that you are using. You can end up with multiple versions of a document, and it's difficult to know which is the most current. If you must have two computers, be sure to use software such as Laplink or Briefcase (which is built into Windows XP) that can synchronize your files so that you are always working with the most current version.

Paper Files

A similar challenge in splitting work between two offices has to do with paper files. Unless you feel like carting everything back and forth, you may need to think about a second set of key files. Ditto for reference materials. For specific files related to a given project, have a way to easily grab what you need. Storing them in a portable file box can help.

Confidentiality

One thing that you need to consider when carting around either paper or electronic files is whether the information is confidential. Anything having to do with medical records, insurance or financial information, classified or proprietary information, or any other information that is potentially damaging will probably have to be left in your office, maybe under lock and key. Before taking any information off-site, consider what would happen if you were to leave it, say, in a train station. Would it be a problem? If so, you'd better leave it at work. The same goes for information you carry while traveling.

Home-Office Deductions

Home-office deductions can save you a lot of money come tax time. If you are planning to take one, be sure to check on whether you work at home enough to qualify for one. The IRS (I'm told) loves to nab people for home-office deductions that are not legitimate. Unless your home office is your primary office, it's probably best to bypass this deduction.

In summary, a home office provides stretches of quiet time, which allows you to get lots of high-quality work done. Merging your two work spaces will help make that happen. Best of all, you'll avoid having the information you need at the "other" office.

▪ 50 ▪
Balancing Work with the Rest of Your Life

Work is important. But while it may occupy a substantial portion of your time, it is not the only thing in life. You will be more efficient in your work if you consider how it fits with your life outside of work.

Realize That You Are Making a Contribution

Meaningless work can sap your joy and spill over to other parts of your life. However, your perception of what you do can make a huge difference in how you think about your work. Having been a part of many different organizations, I take a broader view of work than I used to. It is my firm belief that most jobs are important. No matter what level your job, you have an important contribution to make, even if the work you do does not command the instant respect of others.

Let me give you an example. The position of receptionist is frequently looked down upon and poorly paid. Yet this job is vital. The receptionist is most people's first contact with a company. A competent, friendly receptionist can set the tone for all visitors to the organization and anyone who calls on the phone. A receptionist can also do a poor job and set a very negative tone. It is an important job that does not have a high profile. The same is true for many other jobs.

Understanding that your job is important can help you find meaning in your day-to-day activities and make your job more satisfying.

Do Work That Is Consistent with Your Values

Another consideration has to do with whether your work conflicts with your values. If it does, you are likely to be inefficient, and your unhappiness will spill into other areas of your life. It could be that the company makes something that you are opposed to (for example, you might be a pacifist working for a defense contractor). Perhaps your company is dishonest in the way that it approaches business—lying to customers, stealing software, and generally behaving badly. In either case, your unhappiness will have a negative influence on your life. Recognizing this inconsistency can spur you into making positive changes and perhaps looking for a job that is a better match for you.

Do Work That Is Consistent with Your Life

A similar principle has to do with finding work that is consistent with the rest of your life. Your company may be fine in many ways. You may be doing work that you feel positively about. If your life is drawing you elsewhere, however, you will be unhappy, which can influence your performance on the job. For example, your job may require you to work a lot of hours when you would rather be home with your family. Men and women in this situation often feel guilty when they are away from home more than they would like. The result is unhappiness and inefficiency. Use this unhappiness as a catalyst to improve your situation by lobbying for changes in the type of work you do or the hours that you need to be available.

In summary, work can be one of the most rewarding things you do on this earth. It is your chance to make a contribution to the world, support your family, and use your talents and abilities. I wish you the best of luck as you become more efficient in your work and use this efficiency to create the type of life that you want.

Kathleen Kendall-Tackett, Ph.D., is a health psychologist whose work involves helping people cope with the stresses and strains of everyday life—at home and in the office. A research associate professor of psychology at the Family Research Laboratory, University of New Hampshire, she is also a fellow of the American Psychological Association. Kendall-Tackett is the author or editor of ten books including *The Well-Ordered Home* and the *Hidden Feelings of Motherhood.*

Kendall-Tackett has seen the impact of disorganization both in her own life, and in the lives of people she knows. While in graduate school, she had numerous housecleaning, homemaking and clerical jobs. Since graduating, she has traveled the country meeting with people and seeing them in a wide variety of home and office settings. It is the combination of research interests and her life experiences that led her to understand the psychological stress people experience when confronted with chronic disorganization. She has also applied the results of psychological research to formulate her unique insights into helping people understand the reasons why organization may be difficult for them, and the simple techniques that can transform a home or office from a clutter zone into a serene and efficient workplace. Be sure to visit Kendall-Tackett's website: www.thewellorderedlife.com.

Some Other New Harbinger Titles

Talk to Me, Item 3317 $12.95

Romantic Intelligence, Item 3309 $15.95

Transformational Divorce, Item 3414 $13.95

The Rape Recovery Handbook, Item 3376 $15.95

Eating Mindfully, Item 3503 $13.95

Sex Talk, Item 2868 $12.95

Everyday Adventures for the Soul, Item 2981 $11.95

A Woman's Addiction Workbook, Item 2973 $18.95

The Daughter-In-Law's Survival Guide, Item 2817 $12.95

PMDD, Item 2833 $13.95

The Vulvodynia Survival Guide, Item 2914 $15.95

Love Tune-Ups, Item 2744 $10.95

The Deepest Blue, Item 2531 $13.95

The 50 Best Ways to Simplify Your Life, Item 2558 $11.95

Brave New You, Item 2590 $13.95

Loving Your Teenage Daughter, Item 2620 $14.95

The Hidden Feelings of Motherhood, Item 2485 $14.95

The Woman's Book of Sleep, Item 2493 $14.95

Pregnancy Stories, Item 2361 $14.95

The Women's Guide to Total Self-Esteem, Item 2418 $13.95

Call **toll free, 1-800-748-6273,** or log on to our online bookstore at **www.newharbinger.com** to order. Have your Visa or Mastercard number ready. Or send a check for the titles you want to New Harbinger Publications, Inc., 5674 Shattuck Ave., Oakland, CA 94609. Include $4.50 for the first book and 75¢ for each additional book, to cover shipping and handling. (California residents please include appropriate sales tax.) Allow two to five weeks for delivery.

Prices subject to change without notice.